Mifflin Harcourt

Reading Comprehension

Grade 8

Printed in the U.S.A.

ISBN 978-0-544-26772-5

1 2 3 4 5 6 7 8 9 10   0982   22 21 20 19 18 17 16 15 14

4500460777   A B C D E F G

Dear Parent,

Welcome to the *Core Skills Reading Comprehension* series! You have selected a unique book that focuses on developing your child's comprehension skills, the reading and thinking processes associated with the printed word. Because this series was designed by experienced reading professionals, your child will have reading success as well as gain a firm understanding of the necessary skills outlined in the Common Core State Standards.

Reading should be a fun, relaxed activity for children. They should read selections that relate to or build on their own experiences. Vocabulary should be presented in a sequential and logical progression. The selections in this series build on these philosophies to insure your child's reading success. Other important features in this series that will further aid your child include:

- Interesting short reading selections appealing to adolescent readers.

- Vocabulary introduced in context and repeated often.

- Comprehension skills applied in context to make the reading more relevant.

- Multiple-choice exercises that develop skills for standardized test taking.

You may wish to have your child read the selections silently or orally, but you will find that sharing the selections and activities with your child will provide additional confidence and support to succeed. When learners experience success, learning becomes a continuous process moving them onward to higher achievements. Moreover, the more your child reads, the more proficient she or he will become.

Enjoy this special time with your child!

Sincerely,
The Educators and Staff of Houghton Mifflin Harcourt

Core Skills Reading Comprehension
GRADE 8

Table of Contents

Table of Contents
Core Skills Reading Comprehension, Grade 8

Table of Contents
Core Skills Reading Comprehension, Grade 8

Skills Correlation

LANGUAGE ARTS SKILL	SELECTION
COMPREHENSION	
Literary Texts	
*Text Evidence to Support Analysis, Inferences	1, 2, 3, 4, 6, Skills Review: Selections 1–6, 7
*Theme or Central Idea; Characters, Setting, Plot	1, 2, 3, 6, Skills Review: Selections 1–6
*Objective Summary	1, Skills Review: Selections 1–6
*Analyze Dialogue and Events; Action and Character	6, 7
*Vocabulary in Context; Figurative Language; Word Choice	1, 4, 6
*Compare and Contrast Text Structures	6
*Point of View	1, 6
*Themes, Events, Character Types from Myths, Traditional Stories, or Religious Works	6
Poems	7, Skills Review: Selections 7–12
Author's Purpose	4
Cause and Effect	Skills Review: Selections 1–6
Informational Texts	
*Textual Evidence to Support Analysis and Inference	3, 5, 7, 8, 9, 10, 11, 12
*Central Idea; Objective Summary	3, 12, Skills Review: Selections 7–12
*Connections and Distinctions: Individuals, Ideas, Events	7, 10
*Vocabulary in Context; Figurative, Connotative, Technical Meaning; Word Choice	9, 10
*Point of View; Purpose	9, 11
*Evaluate Arguments and Claims	9, 10, 11, Skills Review: Selections 7–12
*Conflicting Information on the Same Topic in Two Texts	9, 10
Fact vs. Fiction/Opinion	3, 9, Skills Review: Selections 7–12
Reading Charts and Graphs	Skills Review: Selections 1–6, 7, 12

* Aligns to the Common Core State Standards for English Language Arts grade 8

Skills Correlation, continued

LANGUAGE ARTS SKILL	SELECTION
VOCABULARY	
*Word Meaning	1, 2, 3, 5, 8
Analogies	7, Skills Review: Selections 7–12
Idioms; Figurative Language	1
Synonyms and Antonyms	3, 4, 5, Skills Review: Selections 1–6, 7
RESEARCH AND STUDY SKILLS	
Research Tools	2, 3
Outlines	2, 8

* Aligns to the Common Core State Standards for English Language Arts grade 8

Selection 1

Mistaken Identity

All kids need friends, especially new kids at Jordan Middle School. My name is Jane Austen Street and I, unfortunately, am one of those new kids. A lot of new kids don't have any trouble fitting in. They make friends fast. But I'm not one of them. I don't usually talk about myself. I've never had an adventure in baby-sitting. I don't wear designer clothes. And, I can never think of just the right thing to say when some kid at school makes me a target of a smart remark. Not that I want to say something smart, you understand. I'm not interested in working hard to be like everybody else. I want to be me, but it takes time. And kids like Madison James just don't get it.

The other day, for example, I wore my overalls to school. I know overalls aren't for everybody, but I like to be different. Anyway, between classes Madison yells at me in the hall. I'm standing in front of the principal and every eighth-grader at Jordan Middle School when I hear, "Hey, Farmer Street, where's your cow?" I knew I was as red as a late summer tomato because I could feel my face burning. I didn't say anything. Instead, I smiled a pathetic smile and slipped away like I didn't exist.

For the moment, Madison James is my living nightmare. She's the eyelash on my contact lens. She's the dried blob in my hair gel. She's the…the…well, you get the idea. Ever since I moved across town to Jordan Middle School, Madison has been a pain in my side.

First thing every morning, I look at Madison. She's in Ms. Mitchell's first-period English class just like me. Madison is also the last person I see every day. That's because she and I are in gym last period. She's everywhere I am and everywhere I look. And, she's everything I'm not and everything I don't want to be. She looks like she just stepped out of a magazine. You know what I mean. She's shiny and glossy and, well, together. She's popular and she knows it. She doesn't talk to me unless she has something nasty to say. And she doesn't look at me without squinting. Her eyes practically disappear into hateful lines across her face.

I wasn't surprised when Madison's attention turned to my name. In fact, I was surprised it hadn't happened sooner. Ms. Mitchell started it when she passed out copies of *Pride and Prejudice*. The writer's name is the same as mine—Jane Austen. Obviously, that's not my fault. But as soon as Madison heard the name, she blurted, "Jane Austen? That's your name."

I rolled my eyes, hoping the rest of the class would think that Madison's observation was too obvious, if you know what I mean. "She's my mother's favorite author," I answered casually, pretending that the matter wasn't worth discussing. What I wasn't willing to say was that I like Jane Austen, too. And, so far anyway, *Pride and Prejudice* is my all-time favorite book. I've read it five times already. But there are some things even I know it's smarter to keep to yourself when you're in eighth grade.

Ms. Mitchell explained that Jane Austen lived more than 200 years ago. Madison swung her head around, zeroing in on me like an angry bee with a stinger. "Your mother named you after a dead writer?" A few people in my class snickered. The others seemed struck by boredom.

Almost as a reflex, I said, "I'm named after a dead writer. You're named after a dead president. But you only got his last name." More people seemed to be paying attention this time. I heard more laughter. So did Madison, who looked, probably for the first time in her life, unsure of herself, deflated. She turned around without saying anything.

When I saw Madison's reaction, I felt ashamed. As much as I hated being new and not fitting in right away, I also hated acting like this. My smart remark made me no different than Madison. But I didn't have time to think about it. Ms. Mitchell was giving class assignments.

"I want you to read this book with a partner and confer about it," Ms. Mitchell said. "You have one week. Then, you and your partner will present a short report to the class on a topic that I'll give you today. Madison and Jane," she smiled, looking directly at us, "I want you two to report on what we can learn from the main characters in *Pride and Prejudice*."

When Ms. Mitchell finished giving assignments, Madison and I took our pass and went to the library. We found a table in the back. Neither of us said anything at first. Then Madison said, "So what's this book about? You must know if you're named after the author."

"Well," I said slowly, "it's about two people who get the wrong idea about each other. One character, Mr. Darcy, is shy. He finds it hard talking to people he doesn't know. Because Mr. Darcy never says anything, Elizabeth Bennet, the other character, thinks he's proud, or stuck up. When Mr. Darcy realizes that Elizabeth has made up her mind about him without getting to know him first, he decides she's prejudiced."

Madison looked at me but didn't say anything right away. Then she smiled a little smile. "So they're wrong about each other," she said.

"Sort of. I mean, Mr. Darcy is a snob, and Elizabeth does judge people too quickly. But their ideas about each other are all wrong. It takes them a while to see each other as they really are." I started feeling nervous as Madison's smile grew larger.

3

"You mean like us?" she asked. "You acted like you didn't like me from the start. Like you didn't like the way I dress or something."

"That's not it really. You squint at me all the time. And you never stop teasing me," I said.

"Squinting? Oh, that. My mother says that, too. I'm nearsighted, and I don't like to wear my glasses. And my eyes water if I wear contacts. And teasing? I do that with all of my friends. That means I like you."

This time, I was smiling. "Oh, I get it. Then do you think you could like me a little less?"

We both laughed.

"I think I might like reading this book after all," said Madison, squinting at me. "Sounds like the author knows a lot about people."

Suddenly, it hit me. Madison could turn out to be a friend after all.

What happens next?

How do you think Jane and Madison's relationship changed? Write a short paragraph on a separate sheet of paper predicting what you think happened in their relationship. Use evidence from the selection to support your prediction.

A **Underline the correct answer for each question.**

1. The setting for this selection is
   - **a.** a church picnic.
   - **b.** a summer camp.
   - **c.** a middle school.
   - **d.** a high school.

2. Jane is determined to
   - **a.** not be like everyone else.
   - **b.** fit in at all costs.
   - **c.** make the cheerleading squad.
   - **d.** wear designer clothes.

3. Jane wears overalls
   - **a.** to annoy Madison.
   - **b.** to do farm chores later.
   - **c.** to be different from the crowd.
   - **d.** to paint after school.

4. *To be prejudiced* means "to
   - **a.** be proud and snobbish."
   - **b.** make judgments without facts."
   - **c.** make precise observations."
   - **d.** be angry and out of sorts."

5. Jane says Madison is her "nightmare" because
   - **a.** Madison copies Jane's test papers.
   - **b.** Madison acts like Jane doesn't exist.
   - **c.** Madison wants Jane to join the debate team.
   - **d.** Madison seems to be everywhere and teases Jane.

6. Madison and Jane are different in that
   - **a.** Madison never thinks of smart remarks.
   - **b.** Madison is popular and dresses like a model.
   - **c.** Madison has never had a baby-sitting adventure.
   - **d.** Madison is quiet and unpopular.

7. Because the point of view of the narrator is limited, the reader doesn't learn until the end of the selection that
   - **a.** Madison teases people she likes.
   - **b.** Madison is popular and dresses well.
   - **c.** the narrator has a hard time fitting in.
   - **d.** the narrator was named after Jane Austen.

8. Madison and Jane found out that
   - **a.** they both disliked reading.
   - **b.** their parents knew and liked each other.
   - **c.** each had wrong ideas about the other.
   - **d.** English class can be fun.

B Now, practice summarizing the selection. Summarizing, or paraphrasing, helps you understand and remember what you read. It also helps you notice the main idea and important details of the selection.

What happened first in the selection?

What happened next in the selection?

What happened last in the selection?

What important lesson did you learn in the selection?

6

Name _____ Date _____

C Write the correct word next to each meaning. If you have trouble choosing an answer, look back to the selection to see how the word is used.

observation	boredom	prejudice
glossy	confer	nearsighted
obvious	snickered	pathetic
snob	deflated	reflex

1. shiny _____

2. a state of being uninterested _____

3. unable to see at a distance _____

4. arousing pity; pitiful _____

5. a judgment formed in spite of facts _____

6. a person who acts superior _____

7. a conclusion based on looking closely _____

8. to talk to another about something _____

9. an unthinking reaction _____

10. something very apparent _____

11. laughed _____

12. acted let down or let the air out of _____

D The selection uses many similes and metaphors. Remember, a simile uses the words *like* or *as* to compare two things. *The dogs ran like the wind.* A metaphor does not use the words *like* or *as* to compare two things. *The dog was a clown for the children.* Read the sentences below. Write an *M* next to each metaphor and an *S* next to each simile.

_____ 1. Madison is the eyelash on my contact lens.

_____ 2. I was as red as a late summer tomato.

_____ 3. Madison is the dried blob in my hair gel.

_____ 4. Jane is proud as a peacock.

_____ 5. Madison is like a fashion model.

_____ 6. Madison James is my living nightmare.

7

Selection 2

Far Eastern Adventure

I remember listening quietly as my parents talked about our new home in the Far East. It was no surprise to any of us that we were moving again, but no one had expected this to happen. The Air Force was sending us to Okinawa. My brother and I had no clue where Okinawa was until I found the atlas. Together, we searched in Asia, and then among the tiny islands of the Pacific Ocean until we found it. There it was, at the end of a chain of islands below the rest of Japan.

Finding the island on a map didn't make me feel any better about moving. Our family had already moved three times and I was barely thirteen. I knew I would miss Charlie, my neighbor and best friend. Three years would feel like forever. Charlie and I would be sixteen years old before we saw each other again. But, as the child of an Air Force officer, I had already learned that you have to be flexible.

I should have known that these three years would be unusual. My first clue was the summer we spent in California. There weren't enough houses on Okinawa for families, and we had to wait our turn. Two weeks before my dad left, my parents drove us to an air base in California where we moved into an apartment. Lots of other families were living there, too. There were loads of kids my age. I think half of them belonged to the same family. I loved the Mercer kids. We spent mornings at the base pool and afternoons at the movies, where we could get in for fifty cents. Sometimes our moms drove us all to our favorite park where we'd have picnics and spend the day playing ball and frolicking. Even though I missed Charlie, this summer was moving up on my list of favorite summers.

My second clue that this experience would be different from the others came on the airplane. We had left California and were excited to be on our way to Honolulu, Hawaii. We had to stop there first because the plane couldn't hold enough fuel to get us all the way to Okinawa. I had never been to Hawaii before. I didn't care that we wouldn't be allowed to leave the airport. I was glad to be there and eager to see something. Inside the airport, my mother bought two necklaces of flowers, one for me and one for my little brother. She explained that in Hawaii, people give these

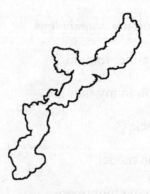

Okinawa, Japan

necklaces, called leis, as gifts. My lei looked like a beautiful
cascading waterfall of white. It was made from dozens of
small orchid flowers. I had never had anything like it. I took
it off before we got back on the plane. I didn't want to crush
the petals. I put the necklace on my lap, which turned out to
be a mistake. Hours later, the plane's humming had put me
to sleep. However, my brother was wide awake and looking
for something to do. When I opened my eyes again, my
necklace was still on my lap. But it didn't have any flowers
on it. My brother had picked every petal, leaving me a string.
You can imagine what I wanted to do to him.

Eventually, we reached the island. We were going to live
on a hill outside the gates of the air base until a house on base became available. We
were excited until we saw the hill and the house.

Tall bamboo grass grew up the sides of the hill and alongside the hill's only road.
Halfway up, part of the hill had been cut away. That's where our house was. Our house
was one of three houses that could fit on the hill. The rest of the space was covered
with tombs. We were living next to a cemetery!

At first, I thought my dad couldn't have found a creepier place for us to live, but
once I got used to them, the tombs weren't noticeable at all. On special holidays,
women dressed in beautiful robes came to pray. Sometimes the women left gifts of
food outside the tombs. My brother and I knew these days were special, so we stayed
indoors, occasionally peeking from a window. Even though the occasion was serious,
the people were beautiful to watch.

On school days, the bus waited for my brother and me at the bottom of the hill.
Then in the afternoon, the bus dropped us off in the same place. Twice each day we
walked down and up the hill alongside bamboo that was three times taller than we
were. My brother kept his eyes on one side of the road, while I watched the other side.
We walked slowly, looking out for the dangerous snakes that we had been told lived in
the bamboo forests. Luckily, we never saw one.

In the storm season, when we had warnings of typhoons, my brother and I helped
cover the windows in our house with boards. We also helped fill the bathtub, jars, and
pots and pans with water. We never knew how long we would have to live without
clean water and electricity.

We also never knew what was living in our house with us. We checked closets for
snakes and looked inside our shoes before we put them on. Roaches longer than my
thumb lived everywhere, even inside the washing machine. It took months for us to
find out how they got into our refrigerator. I remember a time when my mom opened
the fridge and saw a huge roach walking across her fresh lemon pie. That was the last
straw, or I should say, roach. Mom slammed the door shut and went straight to the base

9

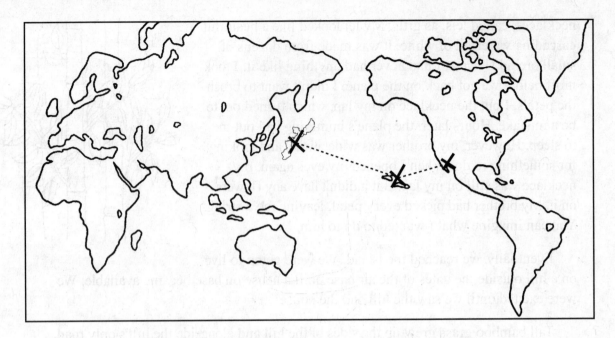

to ask for a new refrigerator. It came the next day. The movers took the old refrigerator away and then called later to tell us what they found. An entire roach colony was living in the space between the walls of the refrigerator.

Our family had lots of friends on the island, but just like in California, we found one special family that we visited often. Tony was my age. His sister Sylvia was sixteen. When we were with Sylvia, we listened to music and rehearsed the latest dances. When Tony, my brother, and I were on our own, we searched through the caves behind Tony's house. Late one Sunday afternoon, as we were saying goodbye, the ground began to shake. We froze and watched our car rock back and forth. The car wasn't the only thing rocking. That was my first and only earthquake experience.

I'm lucky. Lots of people take expensive vacations to have the kinds of adventures we had on Okinawa. How many other people get to learn about holidays for the dead, typhoons, poisonous snakes, roaches, and earthquakes without leaving home?

What will happen?

Use evidence from the selection to write a short paragraph on another sheet of paper. Describe what the writer will be like when she grows up. What do you think she will do for a living?

10

A **Underline the correct answer to each question.**

1. What important thing happened to the writer of "Far Eastern Adventure"?
   a. She moved to Hawaii for three years.
   b. She stayed in California while her parents went overseas.
   c. She moved with her family to Okinawa for three years.
   d. She was a part of an exchange student program to Germany.

2. What kind of selection is this?
   a. fantasy
   b. autobiography
   c. science fiction
   d. informative article

3. Where did the writer look to find out where her family was going?
   a. a travel agency
   b. on the Internet
   c. an atlas
   d. an encyclopedia

4. After looking at a map, where did the writer find she was going?
   a. Hawaii, a U.S. state in the Pacific Ocean
   b. California, a U.S. state on the Pacific Coast
   c. Jamaica, an island country in the Caribbean
   d. Okinawa, an island below Japan in the Pacific Ocean

5. What was on the hill next to the writer's new home?
   a. tombs
   b. an amusement park
   c. an ornamental garden
   d. a movie theater

6. What kind of plant grew in the forest near the writer's home?
   a. oak trees
   b. bamboo
   c. orchid flowers
   d. palm trees

7. What was living in the refrigerator?

 a. roaches

 b. snakes

 c. mice

 d. lizards

8. What kind of storms did the writer's family hear about in their new home?

 a. blizzards

 b. monsoons

 c. tornadoes

 d. typhoons

B **Write the correct word next to each meaning. If you have trouble choosing an answer, look back to the selection to see how the word is used.**

atlas	flexible	bamboo
tomb	noticeable	poisonous
eventually	rehearsed	fantasy
frolicking	typhoon	orchid

1. a flower that is made into a necklace _____

2. a collection of maps _____

3. practiced _____

4. a woody plant that grows in Asia _____

5. to remain open to change _____

6. a violent tropical storm or cyclone _____

7. playing _____

8. something that is hurtful, full of venom _____

9. an unreal story _____

10. clear; able to be seen _____

11. a grave _____

12. in time _____

C **Try to answer the questions without looking back at the selection.**

1. In what hemisphere does the selection happen? Northern or Southern? _____

2. In what country does the selection happen? _____

3. In what ocean is the country located? _____

4. In what region does the selection happen? Europe? Asia? North America? South America?

    _____

5. How would you describe the setting or geography of the area?

    _____

6. What other words are used in the selection to name the area the family is in?

    _____

D **The girl in the selection "Far Eastern Adventure" used an atlas to find out where Okinawa was. What other research tools or experts would have been helpful to her?**

1. Underline the sources that the girl and her family can use to find relevant information about the journey.

    a. a library

    b. an air force base

    c. the girl's social studies teacher

    d. an encyclopedia

    e. a dictionary

    f. an online world map

    g. a travel website

2. Which of the sources in question 1 would you use first? Second? Third?

    _____

    _____

    _____

---

3. Underline the four references that might have the most relevant information.

   a. *The Islands of Japan*

   b. *Travel in China on $50 a Day*

   c. *Atlas of Europe*

   d. Volume "O" of an encyclopedia

   e. the website *www.okinawa.com*

   f. *The Culture and Customs of Okinawa*

   g. *Ancient Korean Sights*

4. The people listed below have written books. Which three authors would most likely give the relocating air force family relevant information? Underline the answers.

   a. Marcus Grant, a mechanic in California, who services air force planes from Japan

   b. Mr. Yamamoto, a professor of Asian studies at the local community college

   c. Kara Lee, who wrote *A History of the Japanese Islands*

   d. Sandra Walters, who published *Folk Tales from Asia*

   e. Jan Willeke, a former teacher who taught English in Okinawa

E **Read the selection.**

Another Kind of Language

Korea is a peninsula below China that juts out into the Sea of Japan. Despite the distance, many Koreans have come to the United States to seek their fortune. By 1970, about seventy thousand people of Korean ancestry lived in the United States. A count of people in 1990 showed that number had increased to almost eight hundred thousand. After the year 2010, the Korean American population was over 1.7 million.

Koreans must make adjustments upon arriving in the United States. They may feel exhausted by trying to make sense of English and the people who speak it. Korean American families also differ from other U.S. families in their definition of what is good behavior. But, because they have a thirst for freedom and a desire for a stable life, they try to bridge the wide gap between two very different cultures—Korean and American.

As employers, taxpayers, and consumers, Korean Americans have helped rebuild many poorer neighborhoods. Because of cultural differences, tensions have developed between residents of these neighborhoods and Korean Americans. Residents who have lived in these neighborhoods longer have sometimes resented the changes the Korean Americans have made. Misunderstandings have occurred between the two groups because of different customs and beliefs about social behavior. Community leaders have gotten the two groups together to promote understanding.

These differences in culture even extend to differences in body language. Body language is an unspoken language that all cultures have. For example, many Korean Americans are not as comfortable smiling as other U.S. citizens are. Korean Americans believe that if nothing is funny, then there is nothing to smile about. They think it is stupid or foolish to smile without a good reason. So, a smile is not always given upon meeting. Looking someone directly in the eyes is also considered bad manners.

To show affection or to touch in public is considered bad manners in Korean culture, too. A simple gesture, like a man taking a woman's hand, is considered embarrassing. This is why Korean Americans do not put things like change into a person's hand. They usually place the object or money on the counter so that the other person can pick it up without touching.

Each paragraph in "Another Kind of Language" has two or more details that support a main idea. Read the following ideas from the five paragraphs in the selection. Label each main idea *M*. Label each detail *D*.

Paragraph 1

_____ Korea is a peninsula that juts out into the Sea of Japan.

_____ Despite the distance, many Koreans have come to the United States.

_____ After 2010, the Korean American population was over 1.7 million.

Paragraph 2

_____ Koreans must make adjustments upon arriving in the United States.

_____ They may be exhausted by trying to make sense of English.

_____ They differ in their beliefs about what is good behavior.

Paragraph 3

_____ Korean Americans have rebuilt some poorer neighborhoods.

_____ Tensions have developed because of cultural differences.

_____ Community leaders are trying to get the two groups to talk.

_____ Misunderstandings have occurred.

Paragraph 4

_____ Korean Americans are not as comfortable smiling.

_____ These cultural differences extend to body language.

_____ Looking someone directly in the eyes is bad manners.

Paragraph 5

_____ To show affection or touch in public is bad manners.

_____ They put the change on the counter, without touching.

_____ A simple gesture like holding hands is embarrassing.

F Now that you have identified the main ideas and supporting details in "Another Kind of Language," it will be easy for you to outline what you learned. Part of the outline has been done for you.

Another Kind of Language

I.   Despite distance, many Koreans have come to the United States.

    A.   Numbers of Korean Americans have increased over the years.

        1.   By 1970, about 70,000 people of Korean ancestry lived in the United States.

        2.   _____

        3.   _____

    B.   Koreans must make adjustments upon arriving in the United States.

        1.   They must deal with understanding English and English speakers.

        2.   _____

        3.   _____

II. Tensions have sometimes developed between Korean Americans and other residents because of cultural differences.

    A.   Korean Americans have moved in and rebuilt some poor neighborhoods.

        1.   People who have lived in neighborhoods longer have sometimes resented change.

        2.   _____

        3.   _____

    B.   Differences extend to body language.

        1.   _____

        2.   _____

        3.   _____

        a. Touching hands is considered embarrassing.

        b. Korean Americans put objects such as change on the counter to avoid touching.

17

G When people begin to learn English, they find that some expressions can be tricky to figure out. These expressions are known as idioms or figurative language.

One young Korean American student in an ESL class said that a fellow student had told her to "give him a hand with the class science project." At first, she felt a little frightened, because she took his words literally. Of course he later explained that he did not want her hand, but help with the project.

Answer the questions about the meaning of the expressions below.

1. In Japanese culture there is a saying, "the nail that sticks out must be pounded flat." What do you think this might mean if applied to people?

_____

_____

2. A Mexican American saying is, "Don't take off con la cola parada." It can be translated and used as in the following sentence. He heard the news and ran off with his tail flying in the air. What does this mean?

_____

_____

3. Sammi looked all over for the machine part and couldn't find it. She thought she had been sent on a wild goose chase. What does it mean if you are sent on a "wild goose chase"?

_____

_____

4. Sarah's mom told us that she "had her eye on us." What did she mean?

_____

_____

5. A Jamaican, or West Indian, saying is, "Keep on the straight and narrow path." What are you being advised to do?

_____

_____

6. A cowboy told his friend, "I feel as low as a snake's belly in a wagon rut." What do you think he was telling his friend?

_____

_____

Selection 3

A Trip to Remember

The bus ride from Dallas was the first sign that I wouldn't like Texas. The rocking bus made me sick to my stomach. Plus, the farther I traveled from the airport, the more depressed I felt. I leaned my head against the bus's grimy glass window and watched Texas roll by. The city changed into small towns, which then dissolved into endless flat, brown, dusty fields. I had imagined places like this while I was reading *The Martian Chronicles*. This was Mars, wasn't it? Where were the video arcades, the all-night pizza parlors, the neon lights, the skyscrapers, and the traffic? Modern civilization had disappeared, and I knew I didn't like Texas!

In a way, this trip started last summer. That was when I met Tyrone at a computer camp in New York. We hit it off from the start, so when he invited me to visit him the next summer, I didn't say no right away. I didn't say yes either, you understand. I had never been outside New York City before, and Texas seemed a million miles away. But both my mom and dad thought Tyrone's idea was great. They were all for it. In fact, their exact words were, "The experience will be good for you." At the time, I had no idea what they meant.

Tyrone and his mom met me at the bus depot in San Angelo. I was relieved to see them, but not relieved to learn we still had thirty miles to go in the Petersons' old pickup truck.

Mrs. Peterson drove the truck down roads dotted with potholes. My head bobbed up and down so hard that I knew if I tried to speak, I'd bite my tongue in half. So I watched silently as the scenery changed from dusty to dustier. Eventually, we turned down a hidden road and into a lane with a barred gate. Tyrone jumped out to open the gate and closed it again after Mrs. Peterson drove through. "We've got lots of animals," he said, pointing proudly to a small herd of horses.

The truck bumped down a deeply rutted track. The truck stopped outside what looked like a soda can on wheels. "Where are we?" I asked Tyrone. He opened the door on the can and announced proudly, "We're home. Come on in."

Tyrone's dad met us at the door. He had dinner ready, and although I didn't recognize the smell, I was starving. Somewhere near the first bite, my eyes watered and I couldn't catch my breath. Tyrone smacked my back, making me spit a mouthful of King Ranch Chicken back on my plate. "This is really good," I said to Mr. Peterson through my tears. The Petersons laughed while I pushed everything that looked like a chili to the edge of my plate. Tyrone seemed to inhale his food, chilis and all.

While I recovered from my near-death experience, Tyrone unpacked for me. It was late and I was worn out. Tyrone could see that I was tired. "I'll wake you up early so we can search for arrowheads before it gets too hot. Sound okay to you?" I nodded and then the lights went out.

The trailer's rocking woke me. Thunder boomed and lightning flashed. In one flash, I looked over at Tyrone—he was sleeping soundly in his bed. Was the rocking of the trailer normal, or should I wake him up to tell him we might wind up in Oz any minute? "New York, I miss you. Texas, I hate you." Those were my last thoughts before I finally fell back into an exhausted sleep.

Early the next morning, Tyrone and I went outside. We wore denim jeans and t-shirts, and he loaned me a hat to wear. The sun was already bright, and the sky was a fresh-washed brilliant blue. I could see clean lines and shapes for miles in every direction. Then I noticed something else. "Tyrone, I don't think I've ever heard so much quiet before." He understood and laughed.

Mrs. Peterson called from the trailer, "Boys, watch out for snakes! Breakfast is almost ready, so come in and wash your hands!"

"Snakes?" I said to Tyrone, stopping in my tracks.

"Yessssss," he said in a scary voice, "sssssnakessss. Rattlesssssnaakessssss." What a comedian.

"I don't like it here," I said very quietly under my breath.

After breakfast, we set off with a packed lunch and a hoe to kill any rattlesnakes we might see. I wasn't too happy about the rattlesnake part, but Tyrone said that we might find Indian arrowheads after the rain.

"What kind of Native Americans were around here?" I asked.

"Lots of different tribes over thousands of years. Comanche, Lipan, Anasazi. We might find something really old."

We reached a gully where Tyrone showed me what flint, the kind of rock the Indians used to chip arrowheads, looked like. He told me, "Head uphill into the sun. Scan the ground and look for anything that catches the light in an unusual way. If you see a rock that looks like it's been worked, pick it up and call me over. If you see or hear a snake, stand still, and call me over."

"Don't worry. I will." At first, it was hard to see so much at once, but after a while, I could spot pieces of flint and chips from arrowheads. By then, even the fear of stepping on a snake had moved to the back of my mind. Hours passed as Tyrone and I moved slowly, inching our way up another bluff. Finally, there it was, lying half in and half out of the sandy ground. I had the feeling that I had been looking at it for several seconds without seeing it. If I had discovered an Egyptian tomb, I couldn't have been more stunned.

"Tyrone, I found one. I found an arrowhead. Wow, a big one."

"Man, that's not just an arrowhead, that's a spear point!"

We started digging. The spearhead was about eight inches long and perfectly formed out of a white translucent flint.

"Wow, let's take it to Dad. I bet he'll know what it is. Or, maybe we can go into San Angelo tomorrow to visit old Fort Concho. Experts there know all about Native American artifacts. You can see the Buffalo Soldier exhibit there, too. The Buffalo Soldiers were African American soldiers stationed at the fort in the late 1800s. The Comanches gave them the name of Buffalo as a sign of respect because the soldiers were brave."

As we started hiking back to the trailer, I cradled the spear point carefully. The silent beauty of the land struck me as I looked out on a landscape that had been unchanged for perhaps thousands of years. I felt small but important at the same time. There were no crowds of people to blend into, no haze smearing the landscape, no blaring radios or horns. Only me. Only this incredibly bright, quiet, bold land. Maybe Texas wasn't so bad after all.

What will happen?

What do you think will happen when Tyrone goes to visit the author in New York? Write a short paragraph on another sheet of paper describing Tyrone's first week there. Cite information from the selection in your prediction.

Name _____ Date _____

A Underline the correct answer to each question.

1. What is the setting for this autobiography?

    a. a bus on the way to California

    b. a train station in Dallas, Texas

    c. a crowded neighborhood in New York City

    d. a less populated part of West Texas

2. What is the mood in the beginning of the story?

    a. excited   **c.** gloomy

    b. joyful   **d.** scary

3. What is the change of heart the writer has in the story?

    a. He decides he likes trailer houses.

    b. He comes to appreciate Texas.

    c. He becomes unafraid of rattlesnakes.

    d. He finds he loves New York City.

4. Where did the writer meet Tyrone?

    a. at computer camp   **c.** on a school trip

    b. on a camping trip   **d.** on a family vacation

5. Why do you think the writer's parents think the trip will be good for their son?

    a. They know he loves travel to other places.

    b. They want to take a trip of their own.

    c. They think he is a little narrow in his outlook.

    d. They want him to learn more about computers.

6. What did the writer find?

    a. a dinosaur bone   **c.** a buried box of gold

    b. an old well   **d.** a Native American spear point

7. When does the writer's mood begin to change in the selection?

    a. the morning after the rain   **c.** the first night

    b. when he is leaving   **d.** when he sees the trailer house

8. Who are the Buffalo soldiers?

    a. characters in a cartoon

    b. soldiers stationed in New York City

    c. African American soldiers from the 1800s

    d. superheroes in a fantasy story

23

B Tyrone tells the writer of "A Trip to Remember" about the Buffalo Soldiers. Both boys decide they want to find out more about these brave men. Follow the directions below to help point them in the right direction.

1. Underline the sources the boys can use to find relevant information about the soldiers.

   a. a library

   b. an expert on buffaloes

   c. an African American artist

   d. an army recruiter's office

   e. an expert at the fort

   f. an Internet search site

   g. an encyclopedia

2. Underline the three references that might have the most relevant information.

   a. *A History of the Army, 1800–2000*

   b. *Traveling Texas Backroads*

   c. *Atlas of Texas*

   d. *Old Fort Concho, a History*

   e. a schedule of bus routes around San Angelo, Texas

   f. *Buffaloes Around the World*

   g. *Famous African American Military Men*

3. The people listed below have written books. Which three authors would most likely give the boys relevant information? Underline the answers.

   a. Jim Fowland, an animal expert in West Texas

   b. Dr. Marcus Thomas, a professor of African American studies

   c. Jeff Bullock, who wrote *You're in the Army Now, 1800–1946*

   d. Amy Wong, who wrote *The Architecture and Occupants of Forts*

   e. Jerry Arredondo, a professor of geography at Angelo State University

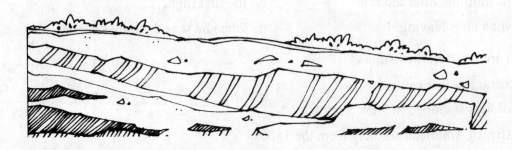

Name _____   Date _____

C **On each line are two words or phrases that are antonyms, or opposite in meaning. Circle the antonyms.**

1. united   eroded   dissolved   disappeared
2. tractor   flexible   eventually   unchangeable
3. exhibit   evidence   hide   unashamed
4. inhale   reveal   expert   exhale
5. translucent   pearl   darkened   powdery
6. unafraid   prejudiced   withheld   fair
7. inflate   recede   deflate   pressure
8. humor   frolicked   sat still   joyful
9. fantasy   blaring   reality   spotted
10. aloof   pale   friendly   embarrassed
11. depressed   abrupt   cheerful   talkative

D **Choose a word to complete each sentence. Some words may not be used.**

depressed	parlor	neon
arcade	skyscrapers	dissolve
translucent	exhibit	flint
stationed	inhale	comedian
computer	denim	chronicles

1. A room in a house for sitting or entertaining is a _____.

2. To be funny is to be a _____.

3. A series of stories or tales are _____.

4. To be sad or feel down is to be _____.

5. Something that is clear or lets light show through is _____.

6. Tall buildings that seem to touch the sky are called _____.

7. A display or show at a museum is a(n) _____.

8. A bright electric light with gases that glow is called _____.

9. To fade or break into smaller pieces is to _____.

10. A business with many video games is called a(n) _____.

25

© Houghton Mifflin Harcourt Publishing Company

Selection 3
Core Skills Reading Comprehension, Grade 8

Name _____ Date _____

E Look at the illustrations of several kinds of arrowheads and spear points. Notice that they come from different time periods and that they have different styles. Read the paragraph and then underline the correct answer to each question.

The bow and arrow was first used in the Late Prehistoric period, around AD 700. Before the bow, darts and lances with large spear points were common. Bird points were probably used to hunt deer and bison since they have been found in remains of those animals. They were also used in battles. More than likely they were not used to hunt birds.

Texas point; mid-1800s

Bird point; from AD 700

Stone Age Paleo spear point; probably Anasazi

1. Which artifact is probably the most like the one found in the selection "A Trip to Remember"?

    a. Texas point

    b. Paleo spear point

    c. not shown

    d. bird point

2. Which arrowhead was made closest to the time the Buffalo soldiers were at Fort Concho?

    a. Texas point

    b. Paleo spear point

    c. not shown

    d. bird point

3. What were bird points thought to have been used for?

    a. hunting flying birds

    b. hunting bison and deer

    c. cleaning hides

    d. grinding corn

4. When were bows and arrows first used?

    a. around the mid-1800s

    b. in the Stone Age

    c. around AD 700

    d. around 1900

5. What was used before the bow and arrow?

    a. Texas points

    b. metal tools

    c. bird points

    d. darts and lances

Name _____ Date _____

 When you research a subject, you will usually find facts and opinions about it. Being able to tell the difference between fact and opinion is important. Remember, an opinion is a belief or feeling about something. Now, read a selection about an ancient Southwestern Indian culture.

The Anasazi

The Anasazi may be the ancestors of the Pueblo people in New Mexico, Arizona, Colorado, and Utah. They were Stone Age people who did not use any metal or metal tools. They made their tools from stone, wood, and bone. More than likely, they were not as civilized as we are today. The Anasazi made tools for pounding, chopping, hunting, and planting.

The Anasazi started building pueblos about AD 700. A pueblo is a village made of stone or clay buildings built next to or stacked on top of one another, sort of like an apartment building. Each family generally had two rooms of a pueblo. They lived in one room and stored food in the other. They probably felt very cramped in their limited indoor surroundings. However, pueblos allowed many people to live in the same area.

All pueblos had kivas. A kiva was a round or square underground room with a roof. People used ladders to climb into kivas. Tunnels connected many kivas. A kiva was used like a church and was a meeting place where the men gathered together to talk.

By the AD 1000s, the Anasazi cities were important centers for trade, culture, and learning. But by the 1200s, thousands of Anasazi began to leave their homeland. In fewer than 100 years, the Anasazi had left behind all they had built. There is some geological evidence to support the idea that a drought, or a time without rain, drove the Anasazi southward into Texas and Mexico. But perhaps the Anasazi just grew tired of their environment and decided to move south.

Put an *F* by each fact from the selection and an *O* by each opinion from the selection.

_____ 1. The Anasazi were Stone Age people who did not use any metal or metal tools.

_____ 2. More than likely, the Anasazi were not as civilized as we are today.

_____ 3. The Anasazi started building pueblos about AD 700.

_____ 4. Each Anasazi family generally had two rooms of a pueblo.

_____ 5. The Anasazi probably felt very cramped in their limited indoor surroundings.

_____ 6. A kiva was a round or square underground room with a roof.

_____ 7. There is some geological evidence to support the idea that a drought, or a time without rain, drove the Anasazi southward into Texas and Mexico.

_____ 8. But perhaps the Anasazi just grew tired of their environment and decided to move south.

Selection 4

Yuki Finds Her Way

The day hadn't started the way Yuki thought it would. She woke feeling tired and grumpy, not the best frame of mind for a ten-mile hike to Blue Hole with the Explorers Club. Then, when she met her best friend, Jada, at the start of the hike, they quarreled about something stupid. Blue Hole was a fantastic place to swim, but Yuki couldn't get excited about walking for hours through thick woods. She struggled to keep up with the others, bringing up the rear of a snaking line of ten other kids led by the club leader, Ms. Reeves.

It was mid-morning when the group stopped for its first water break. Jada sat with some other friends, ignoring Yuki. Yuki felt snubbed and was even more out of sorts. When the group reassembled to resume the hike, Yuki deliberately stayed near the back. "I know this trail," she thought to herself. "I'll take a longer rest and then catch up later." When the last hiker was out of sight, Yuki stretched out at the base of a pine tree. Fingers of sunlight stretched sideways through tree branches to warm her face. Yuki yawned, scrunched down into the roots of the tree, and fell into a deep sleep.

A woodpecker tapped on a branch above Yuki's head, waking her instantly. For a moment, she didn't know where she was. Then Yuki's dry and furry mouth told her that she had slept too long. "What have I done?" Yuki leaped up and started running down the trail. "I've got to catch up!" she thought desperately. Branches and vines clawed and slapped at her as she jogged down the path. Some distance later, Yuki was breathless and felt a vicious thirst. She stopped, holding her aching side with one hand

and using the other to fumble through her pack, searching for her half-full water bottle. Despite knowing that she should save some for later, Yuki couldn't stop drinking once the cool water began to trickle over her cracked lips and parched tongue. She stopped drinking when the bottle was empty.

It was then that she felt the raging fire on her face that would undoubtedly cause her skin to blister and peel. The sun must have moved above the trees and baked her while she slept. That meant that she had slept far longer than she had intended. Suddenly, she noticed how long the shadows were. "It must be at least the middle of the afternoon," she thought to herself. The path she was following narrowed to a dark point. "This is a deer trail, not the way to Blue Hole." Fear bubbled up from her belly as she realized her mistake. "I don't know where I am," she whispered to the woods.

Yuki's tears made the forest dip and shimmer, turning it into a runny watercolor of greens and blues. Slowly she tried to retrace her steps, following the slender deer trail. "I have to get back to the place where I slept," she thought desperately. She walked a while but couldn't find her "sleeping tree." Surely by now Ms. Reeves and the group had come to look for her. Chances were they'd find her before dark. But if they didn't, she'd have to spend the night in the woods.

"Heeelllp! Help me!" yelled Yuki in her panic. "I'm here. Please, I'm over here!"

The woods swallowed her screams, and every other sound, too. There were no buzzing insects, no chirping birds, no scurrying squirrels. She'd never heard such silence before. She'd never felt so alone.

Slowly, a red bird began a sweet song whose notes fell from the tree branches like drops of rain. Joining in, a blue jay scolded, then a bee buzzed by, a squirrel chattered, and a crow cawed. At last, the forest symphony was playing again, and Yuki felt calmer.

She had to get a grip on herself. She couldn't let fear lead her into any more stupid decisions. "Think. Use your head," she said to herself, remembering her grandmother's constant warning to think before acting. "Be an actor, not a reactor," she used to say. There was something else her grandmother used to say. Being positive changes bad luck into good luck. So far today, Yuki thought glumly, she had forgotten everything her grandmother had taught her. Now seemed like a good time to start remembering.

She sat down and ate the last of a leftover breakfast bar. She worked hard to ignore her thirst. She focused instead on trying to determine where she was and from which direction she had come. Then she remembered the reason she had chosen the pine tree where she had slept. It was the tallest tree around, and its top branches were bald.

Yuki drew a line in the forest litter to mark her path as she left the trail to find the nearest outcropping of rocks overlooking the forest. She scanned the forest top, turning in a slow circle. She saw no bald trees peeking above the canopy. She turned again, making herself look calmly at every detail. About a half-mile away, she saw a tall evergreen tree with a bald top crowning thick green limbs. Yuki used her eyes to draw an imaginary line between her sleeping tree and the top of a tree close to the trail. She abandoned the outcrop, heading toward the tree. When she reached it, she stopped and left the trail to scan the woods from another outcropping. There, she took another sighting, drew another imaginary line, and jumped back on the trail. At last, she reached her sleeping tree. Her footprints dented the ground by the rock, and the trail the others had followed that morning was nearby.

There was a chance the kids in the Explorers Club had already come back this way. Yuki got down on her hands and knees, searching the trail for tracks. Small jagged rocks and woody acorns hid beneath dead leaves covering the trail. They punched Yuki's palms and knees as she moved slowly over the ground. Yuki felt the pain but kept moving. The only footprints she found went toward Blue Hole. No one had returned, but that was good news. All she had to do now was wait. She knew she would be in trouble with Ms. Reeves and the club, but she knew that she deserved to be. She also knew that she could have been in much worse trouble if she hadn't started acting instead of reacting. Relief left Yuki almost lighthearted. She went back to the sleeping tree, where she sat in late afternoon darkness thinking positive thoughts.

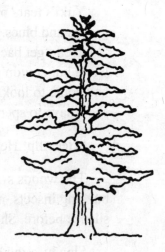

Shortly before the sun said goodnight, Yuki heard the welcome sound of voices. Her grandmother was right again.

Name _____   Date _____

What might have happened?

Think about what you have learned about Yuki. Write a paragraph on another sheet of paper to describe what you think might have happened if Yuki hadn't been rescued that same day. Refer to details from the selection in your paragraph.

A **Underline the correct answer to each question.**

1. What is the setting of this selection?

    a. a bamboo forest with mountains

    b. a pine forest with trails and rock outcroppings

    c. an oak forest with a wide river

    d. a grassy plain with a deep gorge

2. What were Yuki's reasons for staying behind?

    a. She wanted to wait for a different group of explorers.

    b. She was following a beautiful butterfly that had landed on her sleeve.

    c. She awoke tired and in a bad mood, and she argued with her friend.

    d. She had turned her ankle and needed to keep off of it.

3. How did Yuki get lost?

    a. She read the wrong map.

    b. She stayed behind and took a nap.

    c. She followed the wrong group of explorers.

    d. She wandered into an old mine.

4. What is the author's purpose for using descriptive language like "vicious thirst"?

    a. The author wants to show off her vocabulary.

    b. The descriptions make the selection more difficult.

    c. The author wants to improve the reader's vocabulary.

    d. The descriptions help the reader experience what Yuki is feeling.

Selection 4
Core Skills Reading Comprehension, Grade 8

5. What helped Yuki calm down and begin to think?

    a. She had a cup of hot tea from her thermos.

    b. She began to breathe deeply.

    c. She remembered her grandmother's advice.

    d. She saw a search plane fly over.

6. What did Yuki remember that helped her find her way back to where she slept?

    a. She remembered she napped under a tall, bald pine tree.

    b. She remembered what the trail back to her sleeping spot looked like.

    c. She remembered a steep cliff by her sleeping spot.

    d. She remembered a waterfall splashing next to her sleeping spot.

7. How did Yuki know the explorers hadn't come back looking for her yet?

    a. They weren't waiting for her at her sleeping spot.

    b. They hadn't left a note for her to find at her sleeping spot.

    c. Their footprints were all going one way toward Blue Hole.

    d. She didn't hear any voices yelling her name.

B A simile is a comparison of two things that uses the word *like* or *as*. A metaphor is a comparison of two things that are not very similar. The words *like* or *as* are not used in a metaphor. Read the sentences below. Write an *M* next to each metaphor and an *S* next to each simile.

_____ **1.** Fingers of light slanted sideways through the trees.

_____ **2.** Jada and Yuki quarreled like two-year-olds.

_____ **3.** Her face felt like a raging fire.

_____ **4.** Yuki's tears made the forest dip and shimmer, turning it into a watercolor.

_____ **5.** Yuki's mouth felt dry and furry like a small animal.

_____ **6.** She ran through the forest like a wild deer.

_____ **7.** The bees buzzed, the birds sang, and the squirrels chattered. The forest symphony began again.

_____ **8.** The bald tree looked like an old, gnarled man.

_____ **9.** Rocks were scattered around the forest like a giant's toys.

_____ **10.** The footprints were arrows pointing the way.

_____ **11.** The sun closed like a weary eye and sank behind the hills.

32

C The writer in "Yuki Finds Her Way" uses descriptive words. Write a synonym for each descriptive word below. Synonyms are words that mean the same or almost the same.

1. quarreled _____

2. excited _____

3. snubbed _____

4. struggled _____

5. scrunched _____

6. clawed _____

7. vicious _____

8. leaped _____

D Details in a selection tell where, when, why, how, who, and what about the topic and/or the action. Skim the selection "Yuki Finds Her Way" to find these details or facts. Write the key words that help you locate the information and then answer the questions.

1. What kind of tree did Yuki rest under?

_____

2. What kind of trail did Yuki lose her way down?

_____

3. How full was Yuki's water bottle before she emptied it?

_____

4. What is the name of the Explorers Club leader?

_____

5. What is the name of the friend Yuki quarreled with?

_____

6. Describe the strategy Yuki used to make her way back to her "sleeping tree."

_____

_____

_____

_____

_____

who?

why?

how?

what?

where?

when?

Selection 5

Do You Have the Time?

Have you ever wondered how people told time before the invention of the wind-up clock or the digital watch? In ancient times, people used something called a sundial, or shadow clock, for keeping time. The first sundial was probably just a simple pole or stick in the ground. People looked at the direction and length of the shadow cast by the stick to determine the time of day.

You may have observed that at sunrise your shadow is very long. In fact, it's longer than you are. And you may have seen that at sunset your shadow is long, too. But it points the other way. In the middle of the day, the sun is highest in the sky. Then your shadow is very short. It looks like a small dark spot around your feet.

Think of yourself as the pin of a sundial. As the pin, you cast a shadow. The pin on a sundial works the same way. The pin sits in the middle of a flat plate, which is marked with hours of the day. The directions North and South are marked on the plate.

The pin's shadow changes throughout the day. The length of the shadow depends on the height and angle of the sun. As the sun moves across the sky, the pin's shadow falls on each hour of the day, showing the time.

By 2000 BC, people in Egypt and China were making sundials that could be carried from place to place. More advanced forms of the sundial were developed by the Greeks and Romans around 600 BC. They created bowl-shaped dials with hour lines marked in the hollow of the bowl. The Romans even made sundials that could be worn as rings or on wristbands. There was one problem, though. There were no shadows on cloudy days, making it hard to tell the time from season to season.

You can make your own sundial with just a few simple materials. They include:

- a watch or clock
- glue
- a paper plate
- a long, sharpened pencil
- a ruler
- an empty thread spool
- a compass
- a marker

After you gather the necessary materials, you are ready to make a sundial. First, glue the spool to the middle of the paper plate. Then, stand the long, sharpened pencil in the hole of the spool, with the pencil's eraser on the bottom. This pencil is your pin. (Be careful when working with the sharpened pencil to avoid injuring your eyes or skin.) Next, use the marker to draw a mark anywhere on the edge of the plate. Label this mark with an *S* for south. This mark will be used to align your sundial with Earth's axis.

Find a window or a spot outdoors that is in full sunlight all day. Put the sundial in this sunny spot after sunrise. Then, use a compass to make sure the *S* label points south. This label keeps your sundial in the same relationship to Earth and the sun all day long. When your watch reaches the nearest hour, use the ruler to draw a straight line along the length of the shadow cast by the pin. Label the hour next to the line you drew. For example, when your watch reads 8 a.m., draw your line along the pin's shadow and label it 8 a.m. Hint: To make the paper plate easier to draw on, you may want to place it on a hard surface, like a clipboard.

Repeat this step every hour, keeping the *S* label pointing south. Check the time, draw along the pin's shadow, and label the line with the hour. The last line you draw on your sundial is the last hour before the sun sets.

When you have a line for each hour of sunlight, your sundial is finished. You can put it anywhere in the sun, making sure the *S* label always points south. The pin's shadow will point to the hour of the day.

You can make your sundial more permanent by using a cement stepping stone instead of a paper plate. Use your imagination! Decorate the lines on the dial with bits of tile or small stones. Paint the spool and pencil with an enamel paint to make them weatherproof. Follow the example of early Romans and use Roman numerals to mark the hours. Place your finished sundial in a garden spot and always know what time it is. Unless, of course, it rains.

How would you decorate your sundial?

Write a description on another sheet of paper of how you would decorate your sundial. Include in your description where you would place your sundial. Provide a drawing of your sundial to go along with the description.

37

Name _____ Date _____

A Underline the correct answer to each question.

1. How would you classify "Do You Have the Time?"

   a. as a descriptive selection   **c.** as a biography and a short report

   b. as an autobiography   **d.** as a report and a how-to paper

2. What is another name for a sundial?

   a. shadow clock   **c.** ring clock

   b. pin clock   **d.** wristwatch

3. In this paper, the writer uses words like first, next, and then. Why?

   a. The writer uses these words to show how ancient people invented the sundial.

   b. The writer uses these words to help the reader imagine the sundial.

   c. The writer uses these words to show the order of steps in the process.

   d. The writer wants to use metaphors and similes to liven up the paper.

4. Why must the label "S" on the sundial always point south?

   a. The label stands for "stick in one place."

   b. The label aligns the sundial consistently with Earth's axis.

   c. The sundial looks more attractive when it is pointed south.

   d. The label means "this side up."

5. How did the sundial change in Roman times?

   a. The Romans made larger sundials out of precious metals.

   b. The Romans made sundials for chariots and horse bridles.

   c. The Romans made sundials that could be worn on necklaces.

   d. The Romans made sundials that could be worn as rings or on wristbands.

6. Why doesn't the sundial work in cloudy weather?

   a. The sundial is powered by solar energy.

   b. The clouds block the wind that turns the sundial.

   c. Clouds have moisture that clog the pin on the sundial.

   d. Clouds block the sun's light on cloudy days and prevent a shadow.

7. Why do you think the author of this paper lists the materials before telling the procedure for making a sundial?

   a. The author is a very organized person.

   b. You need to know if you have the correct materials before beginning a project.

   c. It is important to know if you can afford the materials before beginning.

   d. The author wants to get the materials straight in his mind.

Name _____ Date _____

B Synonyms are words or phrases that mean the same or almost the same. Circle the two synonyms on each line.

1. permanent	length	brief	lasting
2. recede	resume	quit	start again
3. accidentally	invite	intended	meant
4. kindness	vicious	mean	upset
5. fought	made up	survived	quarreled
6. flexible	fumbled	acted clumsy	discovered
7. searched	abandoned	revealed	left behind
8. happy	lighthearted	moody	ashamed
9. negative	affirming	photographed	positive
10. pretend	biography	imaginary	report
11. march	align	line up	mess up

C Choose a word to complete each sentence. Some words will not be used.

digital	reassemble	weatherproof
outcropping	resume	snubbed
deliberately	canopy	parched
vicious	intended	desperately
undoubtedly	retrace	reactor

1. To put something back together is to _____.

2. A group of rocks sticking out of soil is called a(n) _____.

3. To act in a very careful and thoughtful way is to act _____.

4. To paint something so that it is protected from
   the weather is to make it _____.

5. The top of a forest is called the _____.

6. To only act in response to something is to be a(n) _____.

7. To go back over your steps is to _____.

8. A computer image is _____.

9. To have been very thirsty is to have been _____.

10. To act in a panicked way is to act _____.

Selection 5
Core Skills Reading Comprehension, Grade 8

Name _____ Date _____

D **Read the selection below and study the diagram.**

A Food Web

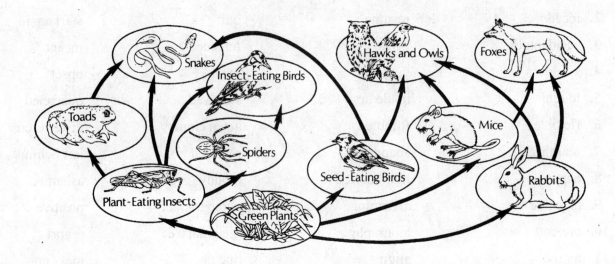

All living things need energy to carry out necessary life processes. Organisms that get energy from sunlight through photosynthesis are called producers. All green plants, such as grasses and seaweeds, are producers.

Organisms that eat each other are called consumers. Primary consumers like rabbits and insects eat producers to obtain energy. Secondary consumers like foxes and insect-eating birds eat primary consumers to obtain energy. Sometimes there are third-level consumers like owls and snakes that eat secondary consumers.

A primary consumer is called an herbivore because it eats only berries, grasses, or other plant foods. Some secondary consumers are carnivores and eat only other animals. Other secondary consumers are omnivores and eat both plants and animals.

The flow of energy among a group of plants and animals can be shown in a food web. A food web shows the energy relationships in an ecosystem. An ecosystem is a natural community of organisms and their surroundings. Ecosystems like deserts can be sparse, or bare, with few organisms. Ecosystems like forests can be rich, with many organisms.

Underline the correct answer to each question. Use the selection and the diagram to help you.

1. Which sentence is a supporting detail from the first paragraph?

   a. All living things need energy to carry out necessary life processes.

   b. All green plants, such as grasses and seaweeds, are producers.

2. Which of the following is a conclusion supported by the details in the selection and the diagram?

   a. In a food web, energy flows from the sun to producers and then to consumers.

   b. Consumers can obtain energy directly from sunlight or from producers.

3. What does a food web show?

   a. all the food that can be found in wilderness areas

   b. the energy relationships among animals in an ecosystem

   c. the energy relationships among organisms in an ecosystem

   d. the food that is no longer available to organisms in an ecosystem

4. Which one of the following is one of the consumers shown at the highest level in the food web?

   a. grasses   c. mice

   b. rabbits   d. owls

5. If all the grasses, berries, and trees in this food web disappeared, the immediate result would be that which of the following would have nothing to eat?

   a. owls   c. snakes

   b. foxes   d. rabbits

6. Which of the following is a supporting detail rather than a conclusion?

   a. Omnivores can be both primary and secondary consumers.

   b. Without energy from the sun, no life on Earth would be possible.

   c. In ecosystems, an herbivore is always a primary consumer.

   d. Foxes get energy by eating mice and rabbits.

7. A hiker gets lost in the forest ecosystem. The meat and vegetables he brought with him run out. As the hiker looks for food in the forest, what role is he likely to take on in the food web of the forest ecosystem?

   a. producer   c. herbivore

   b. carnivore   d. omnivore

8. According to the diagram, what level consumer is the spider?

   a. primary   c. third-level

   b. secondary   d. omnivore

41

Read the following selection.

The Mystery of the Missing Fossil

The day started foggy and rainy. Jeremy was stuck indoors with nothing to do. Or at least nothing very interesting to do. His mother reminded him that he had a report that was due Monday morning.

Jeremy looked around his room for the fossil he was going to use as the basis for his paper. He had found the giant shell fossil the day before along the white rock banks of the creek that ran behind his house. He had looked up some interesting information on the Internet about the kind of fossil it might be. He had found some likely possibilities.

Jeremy scrabbled through the mess that was his room. An archaeological dig might be necessary to find it if it was lost in his room. But the fossil was nowhere to be found.

Next he interviewed his younger sister, Jennifer. She admitted to having taken the fossil. "It was so pretty," she said sheepishly. "I put in on the desk in my room."

When they looked in Jennifer's room, only a bone was on her desk. Where had the fossil gone?

Cause and effect helps us understand plot. The plot must be understood in its proper sequence in order for it to make sense. It is similar to following the steps in a process in a how-to paper. Number the sections of this selection to form a correct plot or sequence of events.

_____ Jeremy took the fossil to his room, logged onto the Internet, and did a key word search on fossils. After looking at several sites, he found a web page that had pictures of a fossil shell similar to his.

_____ Sunday morning dawned foggy and rainy. Jeremy was bored.

_____ "Jennifer, did you take my fossil?" Jeremy yelled down the hall.

_____ On Saturday, Jeremy explored the creek behind his house and found a huge shell fossil embedded in the limestone bank.

_____ "This is great stuff," Jeremy thought to himself. "I'll bookmark this website and use it tomorrow to write that paper for science class."

_____ "Why don't you get to work on your paper that's due Monday?" asked Jeremy's mom.

_____ When Jeremy arrived home, he showed the fossil to his parents and his younger sister, Jennifer. "Can I have it?" she asked, looking at it with a gleam in her eye.

_____ Jeremy grumbled a little and then started looking for his fossil so he could get to work on his paper. He looked all over his messy room, but the fossil was nowhere to be found.

_____ Jennifer was in the living room. "Yes, it's so pretty. I put it on the desk in my room." But the fossil was not in Jennifer's room, either. They noticed a bone on the desk instead.

What happened to the fossil? Look at the picture for clues. Write your ending to the mystery on the lines below.

_____

_____

_____

_____

_____

_____

_____

_____

43

Selection 6

The Gift of the Magi
by O. Henry

One dollar and eighty-seven cents. That was all. And 60 cents of it was in pennies. Pennies saved one and two at a time by bulldozing the grocer and the vegetable man and the butcher until one's cheeks burned with the silent imputation of parsimony[1] that such close dealing implied. Three times Della counted it. One dollar and eighty-seven cents. And the next day would be Christmas.

There was clearly nothing to do but flop down on the shabby little couch and howl. So Della did it. Which instigates[2] the moral reflection that life is made up of sobs, sniffles, and smiles, with sniffles predominating.[3]

While the mistress of the home is gradually subsiding from the first stage to the second, take a look at the home. A furnished flat at $8 per week. It did not exactly beggar description, but it certainly had that word on the lookout for the mendicancy squad.[4]

In the vestibule[5] below belonged to this flat a letterbox into which no letter would go and an electric button from which no mortal finger could coax a ring. Also appertaining[6] thereunto was a card bearing the name "Mr. James Dillingham Young."

The "Dillingham" had been flung to the breeze during a former period of prosperity when its possessor was being paid $30 per week. Now, when the income was shrunk to $20, the letters of "Dillingham" looked blurred, as though they were thinking seriously of contracting to a modest and unassuming D. But whenever Mr. James Dillingham Young came home and reached his flat above, he was called "Jim" and greatly hugged by Mrs. James Dillingham Young, already introduced to you as Della. Which is all very good.

Della finished her cry and attended to her cheeks with the powder rag. She stood by the window and looked out dully at a gray cat walking a gray fence in a gray backyard. Tomorrow would be Christmas Day, and she had only $1.87 with which to buy Jim a present. She had been saving every penny she could for months, with this result. Twenty dollars a week doesn't go far. Expenses had been greater than she had calculated. They always are. Only $1.87 to buy a present for Jim. Her Jim. Many a happy hour she had spent planning for something nice for him. Something fine and rare and sterling—something just a little bit near to being worthy of the honor of being owned by Jim.

---

[1] **imputation of parsimony** (pär′sə-mō′nē): suggestion of stinginess.

[2] **instigate:** to stir up; provoke.

[3] **predominating** (prĭ-dŏm′ə-nā′tĭng): most important or frequent.

[4] **mendicancy** (mĕn′dĭ-kən-sē) squad: a police unit assigned to arrest beggars. The author here is making a play on the word beggar, used earlier in the sentence to mean "make inadequate."

[5] **vestibule** (vĕs′tə-byōōl′): a small entryway within a building.

[6] **appertaining** (ăp′ər-tā′nĭng): belonging as a part; attached.

Name _____ Date _____

There was a pier glass[7] between the windows of the room. Perhaps you have seen a pier glass in an $8 flat. A very thin and very agile[8] person may, by observing his reflection in a rapid sequence of longitudinal strips, obtain a fairly accurate conception of his looks. Della, being slender, had mastered the art.

Suddenly, she whirled from the window and stood before the glass. Her eyes were shining brilliantly, but her face had lost its color within twenty seconds. Rapidly she pulled down her hair and let it fall to its full length.

Now, there were two possessions of the James Dillingham Youngs in which they both took a mighty pride. One was Jim's gold watch that had been his father's and his grandfather's. The other was Della's hair. Had the Queen of Sheba[9] lived in the flat across the air shaft, Della would have let her hair hang out the window some day to dry and mocked at Her Majesty's jewels and gifts. Had King Solomon[10] been the janitor, with all his treasures piled up in the basement, Jim would have pulled out his watch every time he passed, just to see him pluck at his beard from envy.

So now Della's beautiful hair fell about her, rippling and shining like a cascade[11] of brown waters. It reached below her knee and made itself almost a garment for her. And then she did it up again nervously and quickly. Once she faltered for a minute and stood still while a tear or two splashed on the worn red carpet.

On went her old brown jacket; on went her old brown hat. With a whirl of skirts and with the brilliant sparkle still in her eyes, she fluttered out the door and down the stairs to the street.

Where she stopped, the sign read "Mme. Sofronie. Hair Goods of All Kinds." One flight up Della ran and collected herself, panting, before Madame, large, too white, chilly, and hardly looking the "Sofronie."

"Will you buy my hair?" asked Della.

"I buy hair," said Madame. "Take yer hat off and let's have a sight at the looks of it."

Down rippled the brown cascade.

"Twenty dollars," said Madame, lifting the mass with a practiced hand.

"Give it to me quick," said Della.

Oh, and the next two hours tripped by on rosy wings. Forget the hashed metaphor. She was ransacking the stores for Jim's present.

---

[7] **pier glass:** a narrow mirror set in a wall section between windows.
[8] **agile** (ăj´əl): able to move quickly and easily. Suddenly, she whirled from the window and stood before the glass. Her eyes were shining brilliantly, but her face had lost its color within twenty seconds. Rapidly she pulled down her hair and let it fall to its full length.
[9] **Queen of Sheba:** in the Bible, a rich Arabian queen.
[10] **King Solomon:** a biblical king of Israel, known for his wisdom and wealth.
[11] **cascade** (kă-skād´): waterfall.

45

© Houghton Mifflin Harcourt Publishing Company

Selection 6
Core Skills Reading Comprehension, Grade 8

She found it at last. It surely had been made for Jim and no one else. There was none other like it in any of the stores, and she had turned all of them inside out. It was a platinum fob chain[12] simple and chaste in design, properly proclaiming its value by substance alone and not by meretricious ornamentation[13] —as all good things should do. It was even worthy of The Watch. As soon as she saw it, she knew that it must be Jim's. It was like him. Quietness and value—the description applied to both. Twenty-one dollars they took from her for it, and she hurried home with the 87 cents. With that chain on his watch Jim might be properly anxious about the time in any company. Grand as the watch was, he sometimes looked at it on the sly on account of the old leather strap that he used in place of a chain.

When Della reached home, her intoxication gave way a little to prudence[14] and reason. She got out her curling irons and lighted the gas and went to work repairing the ravages made by generosity added to love. Which is always a tremendous task, dear friends—a mammoth task.

Within forty minutes her head was covered with tiny, close-lying curls that made her look wonderfully like a truant schoolboy. She looked at her reflection in the mirror long, carefully, critically.

"If Jim doesn't kill me," she said to herself, "before he takes a second look at me, he'll say I look like a Coney Island chorus girl. But what could I do—oh, what could I do with a dollar and eighty-seven cents!"

At 7 o'clock the coffee was made, and the frying pan was on the back of the stove hot and ready to cook the chops.

Jim was never late. Della doubled the fob chain in her hand and sat on the corner of the table near the door that he always entered. Then she heard his step on the stair away down on the first flight, and she turned white for just a moment. She had a habit of saying little silent prayers about the simplest everyday things, and now she whispered: "Please, God, make him think I am still pretty."

The door opened, and Jim stepped in and closed it. He looked thin and very serious. Poor fellow, he was only twenty-two—and to be burdened with a family! He needed a new overcoat, and he was without gloves.

Jim stopped inside the door, as immovable as a setter at the scent of a quail. His eyes were fixed upon Della, and there was an expression in them that she could not read, and it terrified her. It was not anger, nor surprise, nor disapproval, nor horror, nor any of the sentiments that she had been prepared for. He simply stared at her fixedly with that peculiar expression on his face.

---

[12] **fob chain**: a short chain for a pocket watch.

[13] **meretricious** (mĕr´ĭ-trĭsh´əs) ornamentation: cheap, gaudy decoration.

When Della reached home, her intoxication gave way a little to prudence[14] and reason. She got out her curling irons and lighted the gas and went to work repairing the ravages made by generosity added to love. Which is always a tremendous task, dear friends—a mammoth task.

Della wriggled off the table and went for him.

"Jim, darling," she cried, "don't look at me that way. I had my hair cut off and sold it because I couldn't have lived through Christmas without giving you a present. It'll grow again—you won't mind, will you? I just had to do it. My hair grows awfully fast. Say 'Merry Christmas!' Jim, and let's be happy. You don't know what a nice—what a beautiful, nice gift I've got for you.

"You've cut off your hair?" asked Jim, laboriously, as if he had not arrived at that patent fact yet even after the hardest mental labor.

"Cut it off and sold it," said Della. "Don't you like me just as well, anyhow? I'm me without my hair, ain't I?"

Jim looked about the room curiously.

"You say your hair is gone?" he said, with an air almost of idiocy.

"You needn't look for it," said Della. "It's sold, I tell you—sold and gone too. It's Christmas Eve, boy. Be good to me, for it went for you. Maybe the hairs of my head were numbered," she went on with a sudden serious sweetness, "but nobody could ever count my love for you. Shall I put the chops on, Jim?"

Out of his trance Jim seemed to quickly wake. He enfolded his Della. For ten seconds let us regard with discreet scrutiny[15] some inconsequential[16] object in the other direction. Eight dollars a week or a million a year—what is the difference? A mathematician or a wit would give you the wrong answer. The magi brought valuable gifts, but that was not among them. This dark assertion[17] will be illuminated later on.

Jim drew a package from his overcoat pocket and threw it upon the table.

"Don't make any mistake, Dell," he said, "about me. I don't think there's anything in the way of a haircut or a shave or a shampoo that could make me like my girl any less. But if you'll unwrap that package, you may see why you had me going a while at first."

White fingers and nimble tore at the string and paper. And then an ecstatic scream of joy, and then, alas! a quick feminine change to hysterical tears and wails, necessitating the immediate employment of all the comforting powers of the lord of the flat.

---

[14] **prudence** (proōd´ns): the use of good judgment and common sense.

[15] **scrutiny** (skrōōt´n-ē): careful observation.

[16] **inconsequential** (ĭn-kŏn´sĭ-kwĕn´shəl): of no importance.

[17] **assertion** (ə-sûr´shən): statement.

Selection 6
Core Skills Reading Comprehension, Grade 8

For there lay The Combs—the set of combs, side and back, that Della had worshiped for long in a Broadway window. Beautiful combs, pure tortoise shell, with jeweled rims—just the shade to wear in the beautiful vanished hair.

They were expensive combs, she knew, and her heart had simply craved and yearned over them without the least hope of possession. And now, they were hers, but the tresses[18] that should have adorned the coveted[19] adornments[20] were gone.

But she hugged them to her bosom, and at length she was able to look up with dim eyes and a smile and say, "My hair grows so fast, Jim!"

And then Della leaped up like a little singed cat and cried, "Oh, oh!"

Jim had not yet seen his beautiful present. She held it out to him eagerly upon her open palm. The dull, precious metal seemed to flash with a reflection of her bright and ardent spirit.

"Isn't it a dandy, Jim? I hunted all over town to find it. You'll have to look at the time a hundred times a day now. Give me your watch. I want to see how it looks on it."

Instead of obeying, Jim tumbled down on the couch and put his hands under the back of his head and smiled.

"Dell," said he, "let's put our Christmas presents away and keep 'em a while. They're too nice to use just at present. I sold the watch to get the money to buy your combs. And now suppose you put the chops on."

The magi, as you know, were wise men—wonderfully wise men—who brought gifts to the Babe in the manger. They invented the art of giving Christmas gifts. Being wise, their gifts were no doubt wise ones, possibly bearing the privilege of exchange in case of duplication. And here I have lamely related to you the uneventful chronicle[21] of two foolish children in a flat who most unwisely sacrificed for each other the greatest treasures of their house. But in a last word to the wise of these days let it be said that of all who give gifts these two were of the wisest. Of all who give and receive gifts, such as they are the wisest. Everywhere they are the wisest. They are the magi.

---

[18] **tresses:** a woman's long, unbound hair.

[19] **coveted** (kŭv´ĭt-ĭd): greedily wished for.

[20] **adornments:** things intended to beautify; ornaments.

[21] **chronicle** (krŏn´ĭ-kəl): a record of events.

Were they wise or foolish?

O. Henry compares Della and Jim to the Magi, the three wise men who visited the baby Jesus in the Christian tradition. How are Della and Jim wise like the magi? Use details from the selection to support your response. Use another sheet of paper.

Selection 6
Core Skills Reading Comprehension, Grade 8

A **Underline the correct answer to each question.**

1. What do the gifts in this selection tell you about the characters?

   a. They are generous.   **c.** They are uncaring.

   b. They are greedy.   **d.** They are sensible.

2. How does the author use point of view to create suspense?

   a. The reader doesn't know why Jim reacts so strangely to his gift.

   b. The reader doesn't know why Della cuts her hair.

   c. The reader doesn't know where the couple live.

   d. The reader doesn't know what Della bought Jim.

3. What does Della say to comfort herself after seeing the hair combs?

   a. "Nobody could ever count my love for you."

   b. "I look like a Coney Island chorus girl."

   c. "It's sold, I tell you—sold and gone."

   d. "My hair grows so fast, Jim!"

4. Which of these is a theme of this selection?

   a. Foolish people make bad decisions.

   b. People who are in love make sacrifices for each other.

   c. Buying gifts is foolish, especially when you are poor.

   d. Only expensive gifts have value.

5. What inference can you make from the selection?

   a. The couple were once very wealthy.

   b. Jim makes less money than he used to.

   c. Della often spends thoughtlessly.

   d. Della is older than Jim.

6. Which of these is true of the couple?

   a. They care deeply for each other.

   b. They have been married a long time.

   c. They both have jobs.

   d. They do not care much for each other.

7. Which words from the selection tell you how Jim and Della feel about his watch and her hair?

   a. something nice   **c.** mighty pride

   b. shining brilliantly   **d.** brilliant sparkle

B **Read the sentences from the selection. Use context to help you figure out the meaning of the underlined word. Then circle the correct meaning.**

1. *"You've cut off your hair?" asked Jim, underline{laboriously}, as if he had not arrived at that patent fact yet even after the hardest mental labor.*

   a. with difficulty   **c.** asking repeatedly

   b. in an eager manner   **d.** in a shy manner

2. *The "Dillingham" had been flung to the breeze during a former period of underline{prosperity} when its possessor was being paid $30 per week. Now, when the income was shrunk to $20. . . .*

   a. sickness   **c.** hunger

   b. wealth   **d.** happiness

3. *It was not anger, nor surprise, nor disapproval, nor horror, nor any of the underline{sentiments} that she had been prepared for.*

   a. actions   **c.** words

   b. feelings   **d.** styles

C **Find two phrases (groups of words) or two sentences from the selection that support each statement below.**

Della and Jim love each other.

_____

_____

Della and Jim are young.

_____

_____

The narrator likes Della and Jim.

_____

_____

Della and Jim are poor.

_____

_____

Name _____ Date _____

D Read "To My Dear and Loving Husband." Then answer questions about the poem and "The Gift of the Magi."

To My Dear and Loving Husband

by Anne Bradstreet

If ever two were one, then surely we.
If ever man were lov'd by wife, then thee;
If ever wife was happy in a man,
Compare with me ye women if you can.
I prize thy love more than whole Mines of gold,
Or all the riches that the East doth hold.
My love is such that Rivers cannot quench,
Nor ought but love from thee give recompense[1].
Thy love is such I can no way repay;
The heavens reward thee manifold[2] I pray.
Then while we live, in love let's so persever[3],
That when we live no more, we may live ever.

---

[1] **recompense:** repayment.
[2] **manifold:** in many ways.
[3] **persever:** continue.

1. What elements tell you "The Gift of the Magi" is a short story and "To My Dear and Loving Husband" is a poem?

   _____

   _____

2. Which lines from "To My Dear and Loving Husband" express the theme "Love is more important than riches"?

   _____

   _____

3. Which events or ideas in "The Gift of the Magi" express the theme "Love is more important than riches"?

   _____

   _____

4. Which words below express the tone of both works? Circle the correct ones.

   thoughtful   regretful   lighthearted   formal
   silly   hopeful   angry   bitter

© Houghton Mifflin Harcourt Publishing Company

Name _____   Date _____

Skills Review: Selections 1–6

A **Read the selection below. Note the details. Underline the main idea, or topic sentence, in each paragraph. Then answer the questions.**

Captured Memories

A unique way to capture your memories is with a time capsule. A time capsule is a box or container that has special items and papers placed in it that represent the time when the capsule is sealed and buried. The capsule is placed in a location that won't be tampered with. The time capsule is opened at a date years later.

Select a box or container to hold the things that you will place in your time capsule. A large glass jar with a lid, a plastic box with a snap-on lid, or some other airtight container will be suitable. You can also decorate your container with images from the present.

What do you put in your time capsule? Find things to put in your time capsule that you think represent your life now. You might think about including things that you know will change over time. Items might include a newspaper, pictures of people who are special in your life, a program from an important sporting event, a list of your favorite music, and any other items that are important to you.

You need to pick a safe and secret place to put your time capsule so that it won't be opened before you want it to be. You may want to talk to a parent about your time capsule and discuss possible places to hide it. After that, make a final decision about where you want to place your time capsule.

When will the capsule be opened? You must decide on a date when you want the time capsule to be opened. The day might be some anniversary, like a birthday, graduation from college, or your marriage.

You might want to create your time capsule with a friend or a group of friends. Make it a fun celebration. Share with each other when you plan to open the time capsule and then put it in the secure, secret location you have chosen.

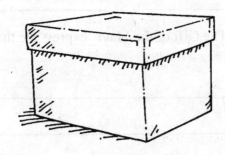

1. What is the main idea of the fifth paragraph? Write the topic sentence.

   _____

   _____

2. Which paragraph makes suggestions about items to place in your time capsule?
   Underline the correct answer.

   a. paragraph 4   **b.** paragraph 5   **c.** paragraph 3

3. What is the main idea of paragraph 2? Underline the correct answer.

   a. Choose a secure, safe location for your time capsule.

   b. What is a time capsule?

   c. Select a box or container for your time capsule.

   d. Think about items you want to place in your time capsule.

4. What is paragraph 4 mainly about? Underline the correct answer.

   a. Find a glass jar with a tight-fitting lid.

   b. Include pictures, newspaper clippings, and a music list.

   c. Have a party with your friends.

   d. Pick a secure, safe location for your time capsule.

5. Which is the best title for the selection? Remember that the title should tell what the
   selection is mainly about. Underline the best title.

   a. A Snapshot of Your Life   **d.** Images: Past and Future

   b. A Party Idea   **e.** Don't Dig Up the Past

   c. Bottle the Future

6. Which step could you leave out and still succeed with your time capsule?
   Underline the correct answer.

   a. Have a party with friends.

   b. Find a safe location.

   c. Choose an air-tight container.

   d. Put items in the capsule.

   e. Tell at least one person where the capsule is and when you want it opened.

7. What would you put in your time capsule?

   _____

   _____

   _____

53

Read the following selection.

Julie was hanging out at the park with her friends. She was running relay races with Jonika, who was also a good runner. Suddenly, Julie stumbled and fell down. Jonika hurried over to her. "What's up, Julie?" asked Jonika.

"Not me," said Julie, holding back tears. "I just skinned my knee, and it really hurts. That soil in the track has washed out again. We just fixed that last week!" The park was in bad shape. The friends had talked often about the state of the park. "What are we going to do?" asked Jonika. "We don't have the tools we really need to fix the park. We need some help with these giant craters. It's like the surface of the moon around here."

"What can we do?" asked Maria, thinking aloud. "Maybe we could write a letter to the editor of the local newspaper. If we could outline the problems in the paper, lots of people would take notice. Many people read and write letters to the editor."

"Maybe we could make signs and protest," suggested Sam. "Then, everyone driving by would see us. Maybe they would stop and join in our cause. The local TV news will cover the story if enough people stop."

"Before we do that, let's send an email to the mayor," said Jonika. "Maybe he doesn't know how dangerous the park is. A younger kid might get hurt here easily. I read online that a high percentage of children are injured on unsafe playgrounds."

The group of friends put their heads together and wrote an email listing all the problems with the park. A week and a half later, Mayor Carson made a date to meet the friends at the park. He met them at the gates with a repair crew. "I want to thank you all for alerting me to the danger here. There are so many parks and playgrounds in the city that it's hard to keep up with all that needs immediate attention."

The friends met the following weekend at the park. They had heard on the weather forecast that the weather was going to be sunny. The park looked beautiful, and the track was in perfect condition. "Let's go for a run," Julie yelled at Jonika and Maria. Sam chimed in, "Wait for me!"

B Draw lines to match each paragraph to its main idea.

1. Paragraph 1   **a.** The friends talk about making signs and protesting.

2. Paragraph 2   **b.** The friends talk about writing a letter to the editor.

3. Paragraph 3   **c.** The friends comment that the park is in bad condition.

4. Paragraph 4   **d.** The friends decide to send an email to the mayor

5. Paragraph 5   **e.** The mayor brings a repair crew to the park.

6. Paragraph 6   **f.** The friends meet to enjoy the repaired park.

7. Paragraph 7   **g.** One of the friends falls down.

C What are some causes and effects in this selection? Write them in the chart.

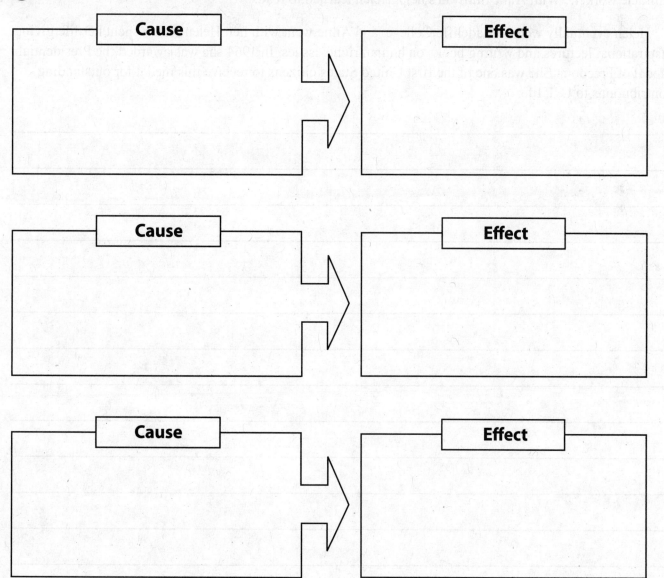

Skills Review: Selections 1–6
Core Skills Reading Comprehension, Grade 8

D **Read the selection and write a summary of it on the lines below.**

Helen Keller and Anne Sullivan

As a baby, Helen Keller lost both her sight and her hearing. She also could not talk, so it was hard for her to let other people know what she wanted. In 1887 when Helen was almost seven, someone special arrived at her house. It was Anne Sullivan, a teacher of blind children. Helen seemed to dislike Anne from the moment she walked into the Keller home.

Anne Sullivan faced an incredible challenge. Not only did she have to win Helen's confidence and friendship, but she also had to teach someone who had no sense of language and no idea that objects have names. A breakthrough happened when Anne Sullivan poured water over Helen's hand and spelled the letters w-a-t-e-r on Helen's palm using sign language. Awareness suddenly came to Helen and she understood that the liquid she had in her hand had a name, water. As soon as she had this realization, she wanted to have the names of everything around her spelled into her hand. Anne had become Helen's "miracle worker." With Anne Sullivan's help, Helen learned to read.

Helen eventually went to Radcliffe College, and Anne went with her. Helen Keller spent her life giving inspirational lectures and writing books on human rights issues. In 1964 she was awarded the Presidential Medal of Freedom. She was one of the first United States citizens to receive this medal for outstanding contributions to U.S. life.

_____

_____

_____

_____

_____

_____

_____

_____

_____

_____

_____

E Circle two antonyms in each group of words below.

1. dull	moody	glossy	painted
2. despise	obvious	disable	hidden
3. panicked	elevated	friendly	snobbish
4. elevated	bored	eager	lengthen
5. wise	sensible	foolish	glum
6. common	regulated	unique	discounted
7. expose	restrict	resign	free
8. reader	pored over	authored	scanned
9. canopy	range	roots	burn
10. elevate	provoke	condense	soothe
11. sit up	delay	recline	sleep

F Circle two synonyms in each group of words below.

1. glumly	happily	sadly	slowly
2. clattered	quietly	chattered	talked
3. reassemble	released	rebuild	detailed
4. scanned	chronicled	serious	reported
5. litter	landfill	trash	lighted
6. chaos	aching	uncaring	hurting
7. pick up	attachment	gather	assignment
8. emptiness	avoid	go around	meet
9. edit	weatherproof	command	protect
10. incredible	factual	fantastic	Martian
11. powered	scrunched	ate up	crumpled

Name _____ Date _____

G Read the selection. Then underline the correct answer to each question.

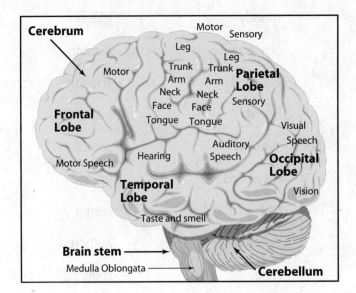

The human brain has three main parts: the cerebrum, the cerebellum, and the brain stem.

The cerebrum is the largest part of the brain. It is responsible for the senses, motor control, language, some kinds of memory, and thought.

The cerebellum controls movements you make automatically, like standing up straight. It also coordinates information from the eyes, inner ears, and muscles to help maintain balance.

The brain stem controls heartbeat, breathing, and other vital functions of the body.

1. What would be the best title for this selection and diagram?

   a. The Human Nervous System   **c.** The Cerebrum

   b. The Human Brain   **d.** The Brain Stem

2. Which is the largest part of the brain?

   a. cerebrum   **c.** brain stem

   b. cerebellum   **d.** parietal lobe

3. According to the diagram, in which lobe is taste and smell located?

   a. frontal lobe   **c.** temporal lobe

   b. parietal lobe   **d.** occipital lobe

4. What part of the brain controls the heartbeat?

   a. cerebellum   **c.** brain stem

   b. cerebrum   **d.** frontal lobe

5. What part of the brain is responsible for motor control?

   a. brain stem   **c.** cerebellum

   b. occipital lobe   **d.** cerebrum

58

Selection 7

Western or English?

Did you know that horses have been around since the time of dinosaurs? In fact, the horse is one of the oldest mammals in the world. Fifty million years ago, horses had four toes and were only eighteen inches high. That made them about as tall as a medium-size dog. Seven million years ago, horses had only one toe on each foot. They were also taller, about as big as modern-day horses. People tamed horses about nine thousand years ago and have been riding them ever since.

At first, learning to ride a horse was difficult. People were always falling off. Plus, they had nothing to protect their skin from rough horse hair. They didn't have shoes to protect their feet from the horse's sharp hooves, either. Over time, this changed. Nomads, or travelers, in ancient Asia invented stirrups, or footrests. These let riders stand up, turn, and duck down. Riders could also use them to make the horse jump and change direction.

Other inventions, such as saddles and horseshoes, let riders travel farther and do different kinds of work. The first horseshoes were actually shoes made from the hide of cows. The hide was tied onto the horse's hooves and left to dry. The Romans were the first to put metal shoes on horses' hooves.

Slowly, riding clothes, or apparel, changed, too. Pants made riding easier. Hard boots protected human feet from heavy horse hooves.

Today, there is a variety of clothing and tack, or equipment for riding horses. There are also two different styles of riding, called English and Western. Both styles have long histories. And both have their own clothing and tack, including saddles and reins.

English riding came to America from England in the 1600s. By the late 1700s, it was popular among wealthy Americans living in the eastern United States. These people thought the English way of riding was the proper way to ride. And riding became an important part of their social lives. People rode to visit friends, rode in hunting parties, and competed in horse shows.

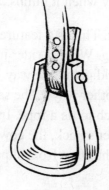 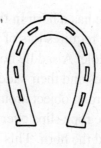

The roots of Western riding can be traced back to the 1600s and 1700s. Cowboys called vaqueros worked on big Spanish ranches in the southwestern United States and northern Mexico. Western riding became more common in the middle and late 1800s. This was America's Wild West period. Cowboys and cowgirls worked hard and rode far in all kinds of weather. Many of them never left the saddle, doing all of their work from the back of a horse.

The ways riders sit and dress are different in English and Western riding. In English riding, the rider sits straight and tall in the saddle. He or she wears a black, flat-topped hat, a black longtailed coat, white riding pants, and glossy black riding boots.

In Western riding, riders work with other animals, like cows or sheep. They must be able to move sideways, pull, chase, and do lots of messy work. As a result, their clothes are more practical. A rider wears a cowboy hat for shade. Blue jeans wear well through long hours of riding. Heavy, pointed boots protect toes and feet from the hooves of cattle or horses.

The English saddle was designed to be simple and light. The seat of the saddle is shaped to fit the horse and rider closely so that they can move as one unit. Also, a light saddle means the horse has less weight to carry when it jumps.

The Western saddle has a horn in the front. This is a feature not found on English saddles. English riding requires lots of jumping. When a rider jumps, he or she must lean forward in the saddle. A saddle horn would get in the way. But cowboys and cowgirls use their horses and their saddles in other ways. The saddle horn gives a cowboy or cowgirl a strong object around which to tie a rope. Imagine a cowboy roping a steer. Once the rope slips over the steer's neck, the cowboy ties the end of the rope in his hand around the horn. This keeps the steer from slipping out of its noose or running away altogether.

60

The saddle horn is also handy when a cowboy or cowgirl needs to pull something, such as a fence post, using the horse's power. Horses used for Western riding are taught to walk backwards when they pull something so the rider can see what is happening. In Western riding, the horse and rider get work done as partners.

Western saddles are built with extra strong leather and stitching. This makes the saddle tough enough to stand up to hard use and bad weather. The seat of the Western saddle is designed for comfort so the rider can work long hours in the saddle. Some cowboys and cowgirls slouch down and sleep on horseback if they have a long way to go or if they have to stay with a cattle herd through the night.

Like the English saddle, English reins are designed to allow close communication between the horse and rider. Reins are part of the bridle, or harness attached to a horse's head. They allow a rider to use his or her hands to "talk to" or control the horse. There are two kinds of English bridles, a full bridle and a snaffle. A snaffle has a single bit, or metal part that goes in the horse's mouth. The snaffle bit is jointed in the middle so it "gives" when the rider pulls on the reins. The snaffle bit has one set of reins. A rider holds one rein in each hand. This makes it easy to control the horse when riding casually or in hunting parties.

The full bridle is more complicated. It has two bits that go in the horse's mouth, a snaffle bit and a curb bit. The curb bit is a straight piece of metal, and it exerts more pressure on the horse's mouth when the rider pulls the reins. The full bridle has two sets of reins, one for the snaffle bit and one for the curb bit. The rider must hold two reins in each hand, separated by the fingers. This allows the rider to have greater control over the horse. Control is especially important when a rider performs dressage. Dressage is a special kind of riding performed in horse shows. In dressage, a rider and horse move precisely. The rider sits very still while the horse performs intricate

saddle horn ⟶

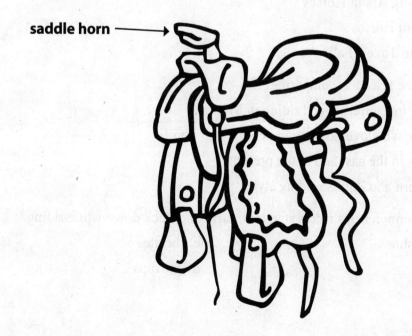

61

movements that look like equine ballet. The full bridle is also used in show jumping, when horses must jump over high fences, hedges, and water.

In Western riding, a rider holds both reins in one hand. Keeping one hand free is important. The free hand can hold a whip to urge a horse forward or rope an animal, such as a stray calf.

People and horses share a long, rich history that continues to be written today. Riding styles, clothing, and tack will continue to change, but the amazing human and horse partnership remains the same.

Which style would you choose?

Have you ever ridden a horse? Would you like to? Write a short selection on another sheet of paper about your day out riding, real or imagined. Include the style of riding you know or would like to learn in your description.

A **Underline the correct answer to each question.**

1. What is the best title for this selection?

   a. Two Styles of Riding

   b. Learning About Horses

   c. Ancient Horses

   d. How to Take a Fall

2. What is the selection comparing?

   a. riding in California and riding in Montana

   b. people who love horses and people who don't

   c. horses in the past and in the present

   d. Western and English riding styles

3. What invention helps riders stand up, turn, and duck down while riding?

   a. horseshoes   **c.** bridles

   b. reins   **d.** stirrups

4. Who first put metal shoes on horses?

   a. the Romans

   b. the Greeks

   c. the English

   d. the cowboys

5. What are cowboys on Spanish ranches called?

   a. rancheros

   b. vaqueros

   c. horse breakers

   d. cow punchers

6. The Western saddle has what in the front?

   a. a rope

   b. a horn

   c. a stirrup

   d. a trailer hitch

7. Why is the English saddle light?

   a. to make riding easier

   b. to help the rider rope a cow

   c. so the rider can lift it

   d. to make jumping easier

8. What is Western-style riding designed for?

   a. jumping

   b. visiting

   c. working

   d. hunting

63

B Summarize the selection by making a chart. Use the charts below to list ways English and Western styles of riding are alike and different.

How English and Western Styles of Riding Are Alike

How English and Western Styles of Riding Are Different

Name _____ Date _____

C Use the information in the bar graph below to answer the questions.

Number of Horses in Millions (United States)

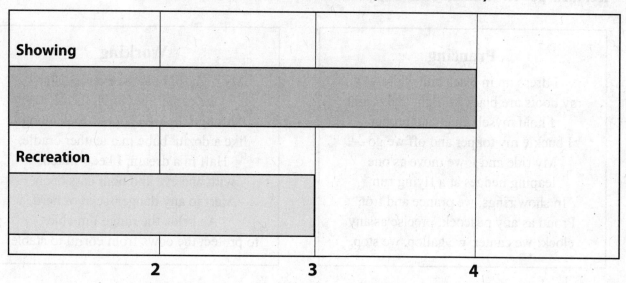

1. How many horses are used for showing in the United States?

   a. 4 thousand

   b. 40 thousand

   c. 4 million

   d. 40 million

2. How many horses are used for recreation in the United States?

   a. 2 thousand

   b. 3 million

   c. 30 thousand

   d. 30 million

3. According to the bar graph, which statement below is true?

   a. More male horses are used than female horses.

   b. More female horses are used than male horses.

   c. More horses are used for showing than for recreation.

   d. More horses are used for recreation than for showing.

4. What percentage of male horses are used for recreation?

   a. 20 percent

   b. 30 percent

   c. 10 percent

   d. not shown

5. About 850,000 horses are used each year for racing. About 2 million horses are used for "other purposes." Would a bar for "Racing" be longer or shorter than the bar for "Recreation"? How about a bar for "Other"?

_____

_____

_____

65

© Houghton Mifflin Harcourt Publishing Company

Selection 7
Core Skills Reading Comprehension, Grade 8

D Most poets make comparisons in their work. Often the comparisons are not stated as they would be in "ordinary talk." You have to stay with a poem to understand the comparisons and feel their power. Read the following poems. Then answer the questions below.

Prancing

I dress up in black and white—
my boots are black as night and bright.
I hold myself erect and proper
I buckle my topper and off we go—
My ride and I, we move as one
leaping hedges at a flying run.
In show rings, we prance and trot,
Proud as any peacock, precise as any
clock; we canter, we gallop, we stop.

Working

My night-light is the evening star—
the cattle's lowing lulls me.
Through the wee hours I rock along
like a dozin' babe in a leather cradle.
Half in a dream, I keep watch,
with one eye and both ears open,
Alert to any danger, seen or herd.
As I ride the range I'm able
to protect the cows from corral to stable.

---

1. What is the poet comparing to a "leather cradle" in "Working"?

_____

2. What is the poet comparing to being "proud as any peacock, precise as any clock" in "Prancing"?

_____

3. What kind of work is the poet talking about in "Working"?

_____

4. What homophone or play on words is the poet using in line 7 in "Working"?

_____

5. Why do you think the poet uses the words *erect*, *proper*, and *topper* in "Prancing"?

_____

_____

E There are different ways you can compare one thing to another. Sometimes you can compare pairs of things to each other. This type of comparison is called an analogy. You need to think about how the first two things are related to each other. Then think how the next pair should be related to each other. Complete each analogy by circling the correct word.

Examples:

a. *Baseball* is to *bat* as *tennis ball* is to *racket.*
   (You use a bat to hit a baseball. You use a racket to hit a tennis ball.)

b. *Rider* is to *horse* as *biker* is to *bike.*
   (A rider rides a horse. A biker rides a bike.)

c. *Artist* is to *painting* as *musician* is to _____. (All the words are alike because they deal with artistic activities. Which word that expresses artistic activities would fit in the comparison and make sense?)

   gardening   (music)   training

1. *Cowboy* is to *cattle* as *shepherd* is to _____.
   sheep   chickens   horses

2. *Hedge* is to *bush* as *forest* is to _____.
   wilderness   desert   tree

3. *Clean* is to *dirty* as *precise* is to _____.
   exact   sloppy   snobbish

4. *Leash* is to *dog* as a *bridle* is to _____.
   cattle   horn   horse

5. *Feathers* are to *birds* as *apparel* is to _____.
   people   horses   fish

6. *Tack* is to *riding* as *rope* is to _____.
   climbing   swimming   snow skiing

7. *Surgical tool* is to *medicine* as *computer* is to _____.
   biology   geology   technology

8. *Dozing* is to *sleeping* as *nibbling* is to _____.
   eating   waking   drinking

9. *Person* is to *house* as *horse* is to _____.
   wagon   stable   guesthouse

67

F Find a word that is a synonym for the underlined word in each sentence. Then write each sentence using the new word.

intricate	precise	hedges
nomads	apparel	tack

1. The measurement was <u>exact</u> because all the numbers were carefully defined.

_____

2. The fashion model wore the latest <u>clothes</u>.

_____

3. After riding, she carefully put away all the riding <u>equipment</u>.

_____

4. He had jumped his horse over the trimmed <u>shrubs</u>.

_____

5. Ancient <u>travelers</u> found ways to improve horseback riding.

_____

6. The well-trained horse made the <u>difficult</u> movements look easy.

_____

G Write the words that mean the same or almost the same as the word *precise* on the lines below.

exact	girlish	distinct
defined	accurate	unfailing
scissored	sloppy	measured
neat	mistaken	vague
abrupt	unvarying	strict

1. _____   5. _____

2. _____   6. _____

3. _____   7. _____

4. _____   8. _____

68

H **Read the two selections below and answer the questions on page 70.**

Selection 1:

Some African Americans seeking opportunity found it in the saddle of a horse. Of the fabled cowboys, roughly one-quarter were African American. Many were of mixed African American and Native American ancestry. Others were on close terms with Native Americans. Many found a steady living in the rough and ready company of ranch life.

In 1870, Bill Pickett was born in Oklahoma, the son of black Cherokees. Pickett left school in the fifth grade and began to work as a ranch hand.

Pickett invented the practice of "bulldogging," in which a cowboy stops a steer by leaping out of his horse's saddle onto the steer's back. Then, the cowboy grabs the steer's horns and twists until the steer's head is turned around. The steer then loses its balance and falls to the ground. Pickett always ended his act by sinking his teeth into the steer's upper lip in the manner of a bulldog, raising both hands to demonstrate that the animal was held down only by his strong teeth.

Pickett's unique skill earned him a job at the 101 Ranch in Oklahoma, a huge spread where cowboys were so talented at the rodeo that they were barred from local competitions. Zack Miller, one of the owners of the 101, organized a traveling rodeo show featuring the cowboys of the 101. Pickett's bulldogging took him to exhibition shows in Mexico, England, Argentina, and Canada—and even to New York City's Madison Square Garden.

Selection 2:

It is told that Calvin Wilson left the plantation where he'd been enslaved and set out for the Wild West in 1866. His reputation as a cowboy spread quickly. People told in amazement about how Cal could tame a herd of buffalo by just talking to them. They told how he could talk to hawks and rattlesnakes, too.

One day, Cal was showing off to a group of cowboys in Montana. He spun his lasso around his head until the loop was as big as a swimming hole. A group of wild mustang horses came thundering up just then and Cal spun the huge loop at them. He caught 25 mustangs in that one valiant throw. Another time Cal caught a grizzly bear with one hand and tamed it by tickling it.

Underline the correct answer to each question.

1. What is the best title for selection 1?

   a. Rodeo Cowboys   **c.** Bulldogging Bill Pickett

   b. The 101 Ranch   **d.** Cowboys in Oklahoma

2. What is selection 1 made up of?

   a. opinions   **c.** metaphors

   b. facts   **d.** similes

3. What kind of riding style did Bill Pickett most likely use?

   a. English

   b. dressage

   c. Western

   d. hedge jumping

4. What phrase best describes selection 2?

   a. a true story

   b. a persuasive paper

   c. a tall tale

   d. a short report

5. What word would you use to describe selection 2?

   a. factual

   b. exaggerated

   c. newsworthy

   d. lengthy

6. What might be a good title for selection 2?

   a. A Grizzly Attacks

   b. Calvin, A Regular Cowboy

   c. Calvin in Montana

   d. Cowboy Cal and His Magic Lasso

7. Where and when do you think selection 2 was probably first told?

   a. in a newspaper

   b. around a campfire

   c. at a business meeting

   d. in a political magazine

70

Selection 8

History Unraveled

Once a plant or animal dies, it begins to decay, or break down. That's how a body ends up as a skeleton. This process happens naturally unless nature or people interfere. Then the dead body is preserved.

A preserved body has been treated so that it does not break down. Unlike a skeleton, a preserved body keeps some of the soft materials it had while the person was alive. These materials include skin, muscles, and organs. In nature, bacteria and fungi help break down a body. They need oxygen and water to do their work. In some places, oxygen is missing. Bogs, or land that is soft and wet, are an example. In other places, water is frozen. Glaciers are an example. If oxygen is missing or if water is frozen, bodies don't break down. They can look as they did when the people died. That's why even today, people find bodies in bogs.

Bogs can preserve bodies so well that bodies thousands of years old can have skin, eyes, and hair. Scientists study the bodies they find in bogs to learn how people lived. Bodies may have food in their intestines, also called entrails, that tell scientists what these people ate. They may wear clothing that gives information, such as what the weather was like where these people lived. Bodies also tell secrets. They tell scientists why people died. Scientists look for signs of disease, accidents, and crime. There may also be objects buried nearby, such as jewelry and weapons. These objects tell scientists even more about people who lived long ago.

Ice preserves bodies, too. In 1991, hikers found a body in the Alps. Near the body, police and scientists found several tools, including an axe, a bow and arrows, and a small knife. The body wore a cape made from grass. It also wore a bearskin cap and leather shoes lined with grass. Scientists who studied the body determined that "Ötzi, the Ice Man" had lived about 5,000 years ago. He probably herded animals in the mountains.

People also prevent bodies from decaying. People in ancient Egypt, for example, believed that after death, a person moved to another world. They also believed the person needed the physical body that was left behind. Therefore, it was important to keep the body in good condition. So the Egyptians embalmed the body, or treated it with chemicals to preserve it. These preserved bodies are called mummies.

While the Ice Man was herding animals in the Alps, Egyptians were preserving their dead. The process, called mummification, took about seventy days. First, the embalmer, a special priest, removed all of the body's organs except the heart. Egyptians believed the heart was the center of a person's being. They also thought a person's intelligence lived in the heart. The organs removed from the body were preserved, too, and placed in special boxes and jars. Later in Egyptian history, embalmers would embalm the organs and then put them back into the body.

71

The body then had to be dried. Priests covered the body with natron, a natural salt. They also stuffed packets of natron inside the body. When the body was dry, the packets were removed and the body was rinsed. By this time, the body was shrunken and very dry, but still obviously human. Sometimes strips of cloth called linen were used to fill in spaces on the body. The body might also be given false eyes.

The next step in making a mummy was adding the linen cloth. Priests wrapped and enfolded the body with yards and yards of linen. Sometimes each finger and toe was wrapped separately before it was wrapped again as part of a hand or foot. Between layers of cloth, the priests coated the body with warm resin that gave the finished mummy a hard, smooth finish.

The mummification process was expensive. Few common people could afford it. As a result, members of the royal family were mummified most often. Using today's technology, scientists can learn much about Egyptian history by studying mummies. X-rays, for example, let scientists see inside the mummy without removing the wrappings. They can study small bits of bone to learn how tall people were and how long they lived. They can study unwrapped skin, fingernails, and hair to learn about the diseases Egyptians suffered and the medicines they took. And DNA samples let scientists make connections among branches of royal family trees.

The Egyptians aren't the only people to preserve their dead. Mummies have been found around the world, including in Asia, South America, North America, and Greenland. People in ancient Peru, for example, salted their dead. They wrapped their mummies in reed mats and then buried them under the floors of their houses. In Papua, New Guinea, the dead were smoke-cured and covered in clay. Then they were propped up so that they overlooked their villages. One of the most well-preserved mummies was found in China. The mummy, an embalmed woman who was an important person in the Han Dynasty, still has her skin, hair, fingernails, and even eyeballs.

Mummies teach us many things. They teach us about daily life and beliefs among people who lived thousands of years before us. They teach us about disease and medicine. They also teach us about the processes of preserving the dead. Whether created through natural or human means, preserved bodies are a link to the past.

What kind of dig would you go on?

Have you ever thought about being an archaeologist? What culture or period would you like to study? Write a description of a dig that you would like to be a part of. Include some of the scientific information in the selection in your description. Use another sheet of paper.

A Underline the correct answer for each question.

1. Why do bogs prevent decay after death?
   a. The bog has a high level of salt in it.
   b. The mud has a natural moisturizer in it.
   c. Bacteria and fungi that break down a body can't live in a bog.
   d. Bog plants give off chemicals that help preserve the bodies.

2. Why is the Ice Man unusual?
   a. He was found with two other preserved people.
   b. He still had his tools and clothes with him.
   c. He was found with a book with his name in it.
   d. He was found in a hut that was covered with snow.

73

3. Why do scientists study preserved bodies?

   a. to satisfy their curiosity

   b. to identify the bodies

   c. to learn about bogs

   d. to learn how people lived

4. How did the Egyptians preserve bodies?

   a. They used X-rays.

   b. They embalmed them.

   c. They placed them in glaciers.

   d. They buried them in a bog.

5. What where Egyptian mummies wrapped in?

   a. grass

   b. clay

   c. reeds

   d. linen

6. What did Egyptian priests coat a body with to give it a hard, smooth finish?

   a. resin

   b. natron

   c. linen

   d. bog mud

7. How have scientists discovered connections between royal Egyptian families?

   a. by studying tools left in tombs by embalming priests

   b. by studying the clothes the mummies wore

   c. by studying DNA samples from mummies

   d. by studying jewelry and weapons

8. Where did people in ancient Peru bury their dead?

   a. under the floors of their houses

   b. in wells next to their houses

   c. on top of their houses

   d. in stables behind their houses

74

B **Read this selection on Egyptian culture. Underline the main idea in each paragraph.**

Egyptian Culture

The Egyptians built temples and statues of their gods. This shows the importance of religion in Egyptian culture. Egyptian people believed they passed into an afterlife when they died. Some of their most famous works of art were pyramids, tombs, and decorations in tombs.

Pyramids were huge tombs built for kings. A tomb is a place where someone is buried. The remains of some ancient Egyptian tombs, temples, and cities still stand today.

Egyptians believed that they needed to be buried with things they could use in the afterlife. Rich people built large tombs to hold these items. Kings were buried with jewelry, furniture, clothing, tools, and weapons. Many kings were buried with full-sized boats.

Some of the most exciting archaeological finds are tombs. Sometimes tomb walls have panels with stories written in hieroglyphics. Archaeologists study the hieroglyphics to find out about the person buried there. Some tell stories about the afterlife.

Paintings cover the walls of tombs, too. Scientists study the paintings to learn about Egyptian beliefs. Much of the art in tombs shows what daily life was like in ancient Egypt. Some of the tomb paintings show farmers gathering barley. Others show servants bringing food or fanning their masters. Still other paintings show families eating or sitting together. They also show children playing games, adults watching plays, and people dancing.

Archaeologists found the tomb of King Tutankhamen, known as Tut. King Tut was a king who died very young. Unlike most tombs, which had been robbed of their riches over the years, Tut's tomb was unopened. The unopened tomb helped archaeologists learn how Egyptian kings were buried. The organs of the king were found preserved near the body and placed in special boxes and jars. The king's heart was left untouched.

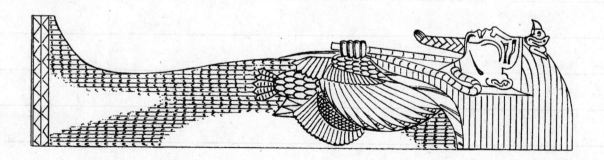

Imagine that you have been assigned a paper about Egyptian mummies and culture. On the lines below, create an outline to organize your thoughts. Use "History Unraveled" and "Egyptian Culture" to create your outline.

Egyptian Mummies and Culture

_____

_____

_____

_____

_____

_____

_____

_____

_____

_____

_____

_____

_____

_____

_____

_____

_____

_____

_____

_____

_____

_____

76

C Choose words to solve the crossword puzzle.

natron	pyramid	sick
enfold	linen	organs
adults	afterlife	resin
riddle	mummified	priest
mummy	enter	Alps
embalm	steam	panels

Across

1. An Egyptian tomb is found here
3. To preserve a body with chemicals
4. Hot, moist air
6. A preserved Egyptian body
8. A fabric used in embalming
10. This salt is used to preserve bodies
11. The opposite of *healthy*

Down

2. Another word for *grownups*
5. Egyptian priests did this to dead bodies
7. Sections of walls in tombs
9. The opposite of *exit*

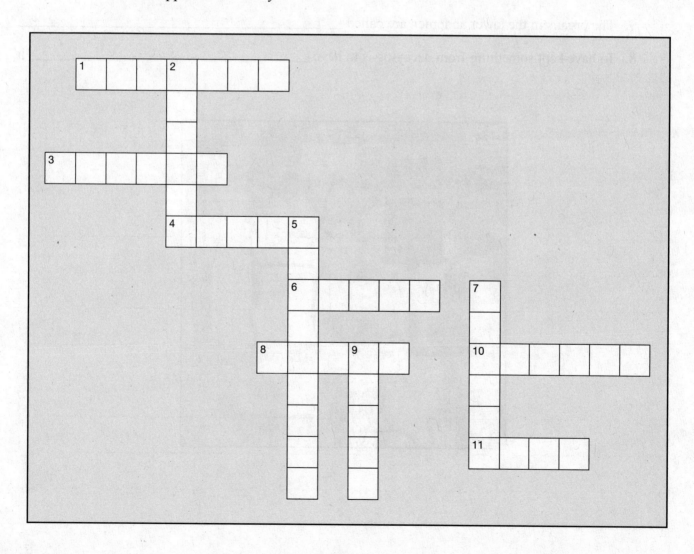

Selection 8
Core Skills Reading Comprehension, Grade 8

D **Write a word to complete each sentence.**

embalm	mummies	resin
process	interfere	preserved
glaciers	intestines	bacteria

1. Egyptian bodies wrapped in linen are called _____.

2. Egyptian priests used chemicals to _____.

3. Huge areas of ice that move as a sheet are _____.

4. Some microscopic organisms are called _____.

5. An action that takes more than one step is a _____.

6. To hinder something from happening is to _____.

7. The organs in the lower abdomen are called _____.

8. To have kept something from decaying is to have _____ it.

Selection 9: Paired

from President Herbert Hoover's Annual Message
to the Congress on the State of the Union

From 1929 until the early 1940s, the United States and much of the world experienced the Great Depression. Millions of people had no job and little food. Here is part of a speech Republican President Herbert Hoover gave on December 2, 1930, one year after the stock market had crashed. Hoover was president of the United States from 1929 to 1933.

During the past 12 months we have suffered with other Nations from economic depression.

The origins of this depression lie to some extent within our own borders through a speculative period which diverted capital and energy into speculation[1] rather than constructive enterprise. Had overspeculation in securities been the only force operating, we should have seen recovery many months ago, as these particular dislocations[2] have generally readjusted themselves.

Other deep-seated causes have been in action, however, chiefly the world-wide overproduction beyond even the demand of prosperous times for such important basic commodities as wheat, rubber, coffee, sugar, copper, silver, zinc, to some extent cotton, and other raw materials.

---

[1] **speculation:** risky financial deals made on the stock market.
[2] **dislocations:** disturbances; upsets.

The cumulative effects of demoralizing[3] price falls of these important commodities in the process of adjustment of production to world consumption have produced financial crises in many different countries and have diminished[4] the buying power of these countries for imported goods to a degree which extended the difficulties farther afield by creating unemployment in all the industrial nations.

The political agitation[5] in Asia; revolutions in South America and political unrest in some European States; the methods of sale by Russia of her increasing agricultural exports to European markets; and our own drought—have all contributed to prolong and deepen the depression.

In the larger view the major forces of the depression now lie outside of the United States, and our recuperation[6] has been retarded by the unwarranted degree of fear and apprehension[7] created by these outside forces.

[3] **demoralizing:** extremely upsetting.
[4] **diminished:** lessened.
[5] **agitation:** tension.
[6] **recuperation:** recovery.
[7] **apprehension:** worry.

What do you know?

Think about the words Hoover chooses to use in his speech. Do you think this language would have been comforting to Americans who were worried about the economy? Explain why or why not on another sheet of paper.

Name _____ Date _____

A Underline the correct answer for each question.

1. What happened in the U.S. to cause the Depression?

   a. speculation

   b. constructive enterprise

   c. overseas growth

   d. a drop in the price of energy

2. What is the best summary of paragraph 2?

   a. Speculation was the only cause of the Depression. If people hadn't speculated, the Depression would be over.

   b. The Depression would have affected only stock brokers if speculation were the only cause.

   c. Speculation was one cause of the Depression. If it had been the only cause, there would have been recovery months ago.

   d. Many people would now have more money if they had speculated. Speculation is good for the economy.

3. Hoover argues that overseas actions contributed to the Depression. What support does he give for this argument?

   a. overproduction of basic products

   b. overproduction of cars

   c. not enough sale of securities

   d. not enough production of battleships

4. What was the result of the overproduction?

   a. poor quality goods   c. lower prices

   b. high quality goods   d. higher prices

5. What other overseas cause for the Depression does Hoover note?

   a. bad weather   c. high consumption

   b. political unrest   d. natural disasters

6. What was Russia selling to Europe?

   a. rubber   c. farm products

   b. sugar plants   d. coffee

7. What was happening in the U.S. that led to the Depression?

   a. earthquakes   c. tornadoes

   b. drought   d. flooding

81

B **Answer these questions about the author's purpose and point of view. Write the correct word or words from the box on the line.**

1. Hoover says recovery has been slowed by <u>unwarranted</u> fear and worry. The word *unwarranted*

   tells you he thinks the fear and worry are _____.

practical	without reason	important

2. Hoover lists a number of reasons for the continued Depression. He thinks most of

   the reasons for the Depression are _____.

worldwide problems	U.S. problems	Russian problems

3. Hoover tells what he thinks are the reasons for the Depression. His purpose is

   to _____.

persuade and entertain	inform and amuse	inform and persuade

C **Write the correct word next to each meaning. If you have trouble choosing an answer, look back to the selection to see how the word is used.**

prosperous	commodities	imported
agricultural	consumption	drought

1. products _____

2. farming _____

3. period of little to no rain _____

4. wealthy and successful _____

5. use _____

6. brought in from another country _____

Hoover's speech includes many facts. Factual material can be proven true. The details can be checked in records or in the words of eyewitnesses.

Fictional material can be based on true facts. However, the author of fictional material might do some of the things listed in the box below. If movies, plays, or writings do things shown in the box below, they are fictional materials.

> - put in impossible details that do not fit the time period
> - include impossible actions, events, or deeds
> - make up characters that do not exist but that act, talk, and dress as if they could
> - include conversations that no one can prove are the exact words spoken by the characters
> - describe characters such as ogres, giants, elves, witches, plants, animals, and people that are unheard of in real life

D Here are some parts of selections. These authors did not intend to write fiction. Some of the authors, however, changed factual material into fictional material that is based on facts. Label each selection *fiction* or *fact*. If the selection is fiction, underline the details that changed fact to fiction.

_____ 1. A map of Earth shows that the land is divided into seven continents. A continent is a major landmass. North America is a continent. But a map of the land does not reveal who lives there. The people may be green Oltrons from outer space hiding among the continents.

_____ 2. The Equal Rights Amendment was intended to guarantee that a woman could not be legally or socially discriminated against on the basis of sex. To become law, a constitutional amendment needs to be approved by 38 states.

_____ 3. The summer before last, my daughter and I experienced a UFO sighting! We were looking out the back door here, and we noticed a silver object coming up very slowly over the hill. It was just sundown so we couldn't really see how large it was. It had red, blue, green, and white lights which kept blinking on and off. It hovered over the huge trees and power lines. It hovered there for about forty minutes. Suddenly the shiny spacecraft took off at a right angle and vanished from sight at a high rate of speed.

_____ **4.** In 1787, delegates from 12 states met to write the Constitution of the United States. Among the issues they faced was how many representatives each state should have in the new legislature. The Virginia Plan, introduced by President Barack Obama, proposed a legislature of two houses. Members of the first house were to be elected by the people. Members of the second house were to be elected by members of the first house.

_____ **5.** States with small populations were worried. Their alternative was called the New Jersey Plan, introduced by William Paterson. It proposed that each state have an equal voice in the legislature and that each state elect an equal number of representatives. Delegates remained split on the issue for months. At last, a committee was formed that worked out the final compromise. Congress would be made up of two houses. Each state would elect two representatives to the Senate. States would elect representatives to the House of Representatives in proportion to their population.

_____ **6.** In 1910, Japan took control of Korea. At the end of World War II, Korea was taken from Japan and divided in two. North Korea was communist, and South Korea was a democracy. But in 1950, North Korea invaded South Korea. When North Korea refused to withdraw, the United States and members of the United Nations sent forces to free South Korea.

_____ **7.** Pioneers often settled lands before the U.S. government had surveyed and sold them. Starting in 1830, Congress passed several laws that allowed settlers to claim land and buy it for one million dollars per acre. Land was so expensive that only a few rich pioneers were able to buy the land and head west. As a result, the West was never settled.

84

Selection 10: Paired

In 1932, Franklin D. Roosevelt gave this speech accepting the Democratic nomination for president of the United States. At the time, the Great Depression was affecting millions of people in the United States. Roosevelt was elected president in 1932, winning all but six states. He served as president from 1933 to 1945.

from the Address at the Democratic National Convention, 1932

Now it is inevitable[1]—and the choice is that of the times—it is inevitable that the main issue of this campaign should revolve about the clear fact of our economic condition, a depression so deep that it is without precedent[2] in modern history. It will not do merely to state, as do Republican leaders, to explain their broken promises of continued inaction, that the depression is worldwide. That was not their explanation of the apparent prosperity of 1928. The people will not forget the claim made by them then that prosperity was only a domestic product manufactured by a Republican President and a Republican Congress. If they claim paternity[3] for the one, they cannot deny paternity for the other. . . .

In the years before 1929 we know that this country had completed a vast cycle of building and inflation; for ten years we expanded on the theory of repairing the wastes of the War, but actually expanding far beyond that, and also beyond our natural and normal growth. Now it is worth remembering, and the cold figures of finance prove it, that during that time there was little or no drop in the prices that the consumer had to pay, although those same figures proved that the cost of production fell very greatly; corporate profit resulting from this period was enormous; at the same time little of that profit was devoted to the reduction of prices. The consumer was forgotten. Very little of it went into increased wages; the worker was forgotten, and by no means an adequate proportion was even paid out in dividends—the stockholder was forgotten.

And, incidentally, very little of it was taken by taxation to the beneficent[4] Government of those years.

---

[1] **inevitable:** expected.
[2] **without precedent:** has never happened before.
[3] **paternity:** fatherhood.
[4] **beneficent:** generous; producing benefit.

What was the result? Enormous corporate surpluses piled up—the most stupendous[5] in history. Where, under the spell of delirious speculation, did those surpluses go? Let us talk economics that the figures prove and that we can understand. Why, they went chiefly in two directions: first, into new and unnecessary plants which now stand stark and idle; and second, into the call-money market of Wall Street, either directly by the corporations, or indirectly through the banks. Those are the facts. Why blink at them?

Then came the crash. You know the story. Surpluses invested in unnecessary plants became idle. Men lost their jobs; purchasing power dried up; banks became frightened and started calling loans. Those who had money were afraid to part with it. Credit contracted. Industry stopped. Commerce declined, and unemployment mounted.

And there we are today.

---

[5] **stupendous:** amazing.

> # What was his purpose?
>
> **What was Roosevelt's purpose for giving this part of his speech? Write a paragraph on another sheet of paper telling about his purpose. Give evidence from the speech to support your ideas.**

A **Underline the correct answer for each question.**

1. What is the central idea of Roosevelt's speech?

    a. The Depression started in 1929 and will probably end by the time Roosevelt is elected.

    b. If Roosevelt is president, he will find out what caused the Depression.

    c. The Republican government and corporate greed played a large role in the Depression.

    d. No one knows what caused the Depression, but it probably won't happen again.

2. Which group does Roosevelt argue should take responsibility for causing the Depression?

    a. the Republican party   **c.** stockbrokers

    b. the Democratic party   **d.** people in the United States

3. In paragraph 4, what do the supporting sentences explain?

    a. when the crash came

    b. why prices dropped

    c. what happened to economic surpluses

    d. what Roosevelt will do to help Americans

4. What happened to prices for consumers in the years before 1929?

    a. They rose.

    b. They doubled.

    c. They fell sharply.

    d. They stayed about the same.

5. During the same time, what happened to the cost of producing goods?

    a. It went up and then down.

    b. It went down greatly.

    c. It went up slightly.

    d. It stayed about the same.

6. What words in the speech tell you Roosevelt is appealing to emotion to convince the audience?

    a. people, fact

    b. domestic, country

    c. directly, indirectly

    d. stupendous, delirious

7. To stress his point, what word does Roosevelt use to describe the consumers, workers, and stockholders?

    a. beneficent   **c.** unnecessary

    b. idle   **d.** forgotten

87

Name _____ Date _____

B Choose the correct vocabulary word for each definition. If you aren't sure what a word means, look for context clues in the selection to help you.

adequate	dividends	delirious	surplus	mounted

1. grew   _____

2. shares of the profits   _____

3. not rational; highly excited   _____

4. sufficient; enough   _____

5. extra money   _____

C What are some causes and effects in the selection? Choose the correct Effect from the box for each Cause. You will not use all the Effects.

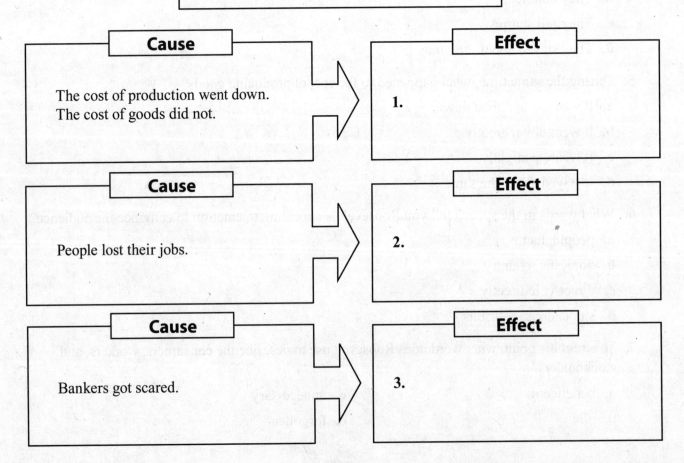

Effects
Bankers called in loans.
People didn't have money to spend on goods.
Corporations made huge profits.
Government taxes were low.

Cause		Effect
The cost of production went down. The cost of goods did not.	→	1.
People lost their jobs.	→	2.
Bankers got scared.	→	3.

88

Roosevelt's speech is partly persuasive. In persuasive arguments, such as a political speech or a movie review, writers often use slanted arguments. The writer presents information in a way that is meant to convince you to think or act in a certain way. Here are some methods used in slanted arguments.

1. **Use of glad words:** words that make you feel positive and enthusiastic about a person or product.

2. **Bandwagon technique:** statements that try to make you feel that "everyone else" is doing something, so you should, too.

3. **Famous-person endorsement:** statements that well-known public figures support an idea or use a product.

D **Read each argument below. Then write the number of the kind of slanted argument used.**

1. All across the nation, it's the Jumpin' Cola generation! _____

2. Rock star Cristina Martínez eats Funky Fruit Cereal every day! _____

3. The new vitamin C skin cream makes even rough skin silky smooth. _____

4. Candidate Fowler is for fair play and honesty in government. Vote! _____

5. Smart people rely on Craig Alarm Systems. What about you? _____

6. Basketball great Michael Trinity only wears GoGo Athletic Shoes! _____

7. Be cool! Be in! Don't be the last one to have one! Buy a Kookie now! _____

8. Go to the beautiful, exotic South Seas! Call Jasper Travel Agency! _____

For each sentence below, choose and write the phrase that would probably make the best slanted argument.

9. People in the know _____ Get Up and Go Motor Oil.

    like   are interested in   insist on

10. Tuna Masterpiece is the quick meal preferred by _____.

    many teenagers   actor Brad Jones   hungry people

11. To drive the Supercharger 3000 is to have a new, _____ experience.

    fun-filled   very nice   safe and quiet

12. The E-Pack Computer has an Ontarget Chip that _____.

    is adequate for games   manages memory well   is lightning fast.

Name _____ Date _____

E **Read the selection and look at the two political ads. Then underline the correct answer.**

A political TV ad tries to convince its viewers to support a particular candidate. It may use several different ways to achieve this.

A camera angle looking up at the candidate can make a candidate seem stronger. A camera angle looking down at the candidate can make a candidate seem less powerful. A camera at eye level can make a candidate seem open and easy to approach.

Close personal space and casual clothes can make a candidate seem friendly and likable. Personal distance and formal clothes can make a candidate seem remote and authoritative.

Some ads try to link their candidate with images that the audience will feel good about.

Short, quickly changing shots can make a candidate seem active and energetic. Long, slow shots can produce a feeling of dignity or peace.

Ads try to boost their authority by using facts, figures, and other evidence. It's up to the viewer to confirm that the facts used are true or are used in the correct context.

Candidate One

Candidate Two

1. What is Candidate One trying to say with his body language?

   a. "I'm an energetic problem-solver."

   b. "I'm a formal, thoughtful leader."

   c. "I'm not sure what to do in this situation."

   d. "I'm friendly and approachable."

2. How does the camera angle make Candidate Two look?

   a. authoritative   **c.** modest

   b. insecure   **d.** angry

3. What images make the audience feel good about Candidate One?

   a. a large auditorium filled with people   **c.** a cute, laughing baby

   b. a group of elderly voters   **d.** a close-up of the candidate

4. What images make the audience feel good about Candidate Two?

   a. interesting signs

   b. crowds of smiling schoolchildren

   c. a group of news reporters

   d. a position of authority above the crowd

5. What else makes the audience feel good about Candidate One?

   a. patriotic images   **c.** the candidate's mother

   b. enthusiastic supporters   **d.** lots of signs

6. What other image makes the audience feel good about Candidate Two?

   a. a patriotic banner   **c.** farmers and ranchers

   b. expert advisors   **d.** the candidate's family

7. What kind of clothes is Candidate One wearing and why?

   a. a formal suit to show authority

   b. casual clothes to appear easy to approach

   c. a uniform to gain the military vote

   d. a costume to appear lively

8. What is Candidate Two saying with his body language?

   a. "I'm a formal, thoughtful, and dignified leader."

   b. "I'm easy to talk to."

   c. "I'm a regular guy."

   d. "I'm one of the people."

9. What else would make a television viewer feel good about Candidate One?

   a. the signs the people are holding

   b. the backs of the audience

   c. the open, smiling faces of the people close around him

   d. the decorations in the hall

10. What might a camera angle looking up at the candidate communicate?

   a. the weakness of the candidate

   b. the strength of the candidate

   c. the openness of the candidate

   d. the friendliness of the candidate

F **Read the ads below. Put a ✔ beside the ads that give you the factual information you need to know about a product.**

1. _____ "The new E-track CD player has cosmic sound effects. You won't believe your ears! The two special-mount speakers will send you into outer space."

2. _____ "The Duster Buster will remove dust and cobwebs from your home with one swipe. As our spokesperson, beautiful actress Sally Sutherland says, 'There's no dust too small for the Buster to Bust . . . try it today!'"

3. _____ "Candidate Al Forest says, 'A vote for me is a vote for lower insurance costs!' Recommended by intelligent people everywhere, remember to vote for Al on November 5!"

4. _____ "Grand Granola is the healthiest cereal on the market. It contains the daily requirements set by the Food and Drug Administration for protein content; calcium; niacin; and vitamins C, D, and E."

5. _____ "'The Super Skateboard will help you stick landings and fly like a bird. Only the best boarders use the Super Skateboard!' says Gordan Winslow, master skateboarder."

6. _____ "The new Stopzits Cleanser will clean your pores like no other cleanser. Recommended by dermatologists and the American Medical Association. Has the approval of the federal Food and Drug Administration."

7. _____ "'The Z80-X Silver Eagle sedan will make you feel like royalty,' says opera singer Cairo King. 'Come in to Aspen's Car Lot and take a test drive today.'"

8. _____ "Try TaterFree, the new lower-fat potato chips. Read the label and see that there are only 3 grams of fat in 16 chips. Write for our special booklet and endorsement from the Surgeon General of the United States."

9. _____ "Read the survey sponsored by the *New England Journal of Medicine* (July 5th issue—page 43) and then give PreventAcid a try. Your problems with your stomach will be significantly lessened."

10. _____ "'The best musical I've ever seen!' says Tina Tharpe, the famous tap dancer. 'I couldn't stop tapping my feet! See it today!'"

11. _____ "'VegoVitamins have all the minimum daily vitamin requirements and a special coating that will protect your stomach lining.'—Exercise Guru, Paul Corning."

12. _____ "The Ab-Xerciser will instantly give you tight abs and a better attitude. Order today!"

G Hoover and Roosevelt had different explanations of the cause of the Depression. Read these statements about causes of the Depression. Write *Hoover* or *Roosevelt* to tell which noted each cause.

1. There was a worldwide overproduction of basic goods. _____

2. The economic policies of the government were not successful. _____

3. Prices of basic goods got too low. _____

4. Corporate profits went up, while prices stayed the same. _____

5. There were political troubles overseas. _____

6. Corporations forgot about the consumer. _____

7. There was a drought in the United States. _____

8. Russia increased its farming exports to Europe. _____

9. Corporations built unneeded factories. _____

10. Corporations had the largest surpluses in history. _____

H Look at the word choice and the length of sentences in each speech. Write a paragraph describing each speech's tone and style and tell which speaker you think is better. Give examples.

_____

_____

_____

_____

_____

_____

_____

_____

Name _____ Date _____

 Complete these sentences with words from the box.

responsibility	speculation	prosperity	fear	recovered
imported	suffered	broken	outside	worldwide

Roosevelt's Argument

1. It is not enough to claim that the Depression is _____.

2. Republicans took credit for the _____ of 1928.

3. Republic leaders have _____ promises.

4. Republican leaders should take _____ for the Depression.

Hoover's Argument

5. If overspeculation were the only cause of the Depression, the market would have already _____.

6. Many countries couldn't buy _____ goods because they didn't make enough money selling basic products.

7. Unnecessary _____ is making the Depression worse.

8. Most of the reasons for the Depression are _____ the United States.

How Hoover and Roosevelt Agree

9. Roosevelt and Hoover agree that _____ was a cause of the Depression.

10. The men agree that people in the country have _____.

94

Selection 11

121 Earhart Lane
Los Angeles, California 90035
November 12, 2013

Station Manager
Space Age Channel Television Studio
P.O. Box 122
Washington, DC 20003

Dear Station Manager:

I am a big fan of your station. I think your educational programs about air and space are great. From one show, I learned that the first person to fly faster than the speed of sound was Chuck Yaeger. In another show, I learned that Neil Armstrong and Buzz Aldrin were the first people to walk on the moon. Now I watch your channel to learn about the International Space Station because I want to work there one day. Your channel has taught me a lot about the history of air and space travel. Even so, one important subject is missing. That subject is women. I've never seen a single program that describes the accomplishments of women in air and space.

Women have played important roles in powered flight since the early 1900s. Let me give you just a few examples. Bessica Raiche helped build the airplane she flew in 1910. Her first flight lasted only a few minutes, but she tried several more flights. Some call Raiche the "First Woman Aviator in America." In 1911, Harriet Quimby became the first woman in the United States to earn a pilot's license. She was also the first woman to fly across the English Channel. In 1913, Katherine Stinson and her mother started a flying business.

Two years later, Marjorie Stinson joined the company. She started a flight school to train WW1 pilots from the U.S. and Canada. In 1921, Bessie Coleman became the first African American to earn a pilot's license. She earned her license in France and then came back to the U.S. to raise money to build a flight school for other African Americans.

I've given you only a few examples of the women who were part of U.S. air history. There are more. And the number grows even larger every year. Women were part of the formation of NASA in 1958. In fact, NASA's very first Chief Astronomer was Dr. Nancy Roman. Margaret W. Brennecke was a welder. She chose the metals and techniques for building the Saturn rockets that flew in the 1960s. She did the same for Spacelab and the Space Shuttle's rocket boosters. Many other women worked with the space program as engineers and scientists. In 1978, six women, including Dr. Sally Ride, joined NASA as astronauts. Twenty years later, Lt. Col. Eileen Collins became NASA's first female commander.

I've left out so many women. And so have you. Unless you include women, you're telling only half of the history of air and space travel.

Besides telling only half a story, you're missing the chance to send an important message to young girls and boys in school. Those children will probably grow up to live in space! This is a good time to tell all of them how they can be a part of the future.

If you don't think preparing children for the future is your job, then you might think about the people who watch and support your channel now. My research tells me that more than half of the people who watch your channel are female. How long do you think they'll watch if you don't tell stories that include them? What will happen to your station when half of your viewers stop watching?

Dr. Sally Ride

In closing, I'm asking you to include women in your station's programming. Tell women's stories to give a more complete history of air and space travel. Tell women's stories to help prepare young girls and boys for their future. Finally, tell women's stories to keep your viewers and your station! Act now so that I can watch your channel tomorrow.

Sincerely yours,

Jen Rumi-Stevens

Jen Rumi-Stevens
Future Space Station Commander

What happens next?

Describe on another sheet of paper how you think the station manager will respond to Jen's letter. Include details from the selection to support your prediction.

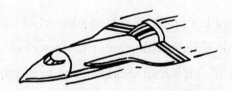

Name _____ Date _____

A   **Underline the correct answer to each question.**

1. What is the purpose of Jen's letter?

    a. to compliment   **c.** to complain

    b. to persuade   **d.** to inform

2. What is the one important subject Jen says is missing from the programming?

    a. men   **c.** women

    b. outer space   **d.** air travel

3. Who was called the "First Woman Aviator in America"?

    a. Marjorie Stinson   **c.** Harriet Quimby

    b. Amelia Earhart   **d.** Bessica Raiche

4. Who was the first African American to earn a pilot's license?

    a. Harriet Quimby

    b. Bessie Coleman

    c. Bessica Raiche

    d. Dr. Sally Ride

5. Why does Jen list so many examples of women in aviation history?

    a. The station has asked her for a list of aviators.

    b. She wants to let the station manager know what she has learned in school.

    c. She is giving support to her argument by listing examples.

    d. She wants the station to increase the number of aviators it profiles.

6. What is one of Jen's main points in support of her argument?

    a. The station is only telling half the story of air and space travel.

    b. The station's viewers are elderly and need more air time.

    c. The station is losing its male audience.

    d. The station is not appealing to the airline travelers in its audience.

7. What does Jen want the station to do?

    a. include more physically challenged people in the station's programming

    b. include more elderly in the station's programming

    c. include more women in the station's programming

    d. include more minorities in the station's programming

8. What support does Jen give for her request?

    a. research   **c.** opinions

    b. feelings   **d.** hopes

98

B Read the selection below about understanding Internet addresses.

If you open the mailbox and find a letter, the person who sent it wrote your name and address on the envelope. The address tells people at the post office where you live. If the address is correct, you receive the letter. But if something is missing or written incorrectly, you may never receive your mail. Finding a website is like sending a letter. You need an address, and you must write it correctly.

Parts of a Web Address, or URL

These letters tell your computer to go to a website. Most URLs begin with these letters followed by a colon and two slashes.

Many URLs include www. That stands for World Wide Web.

http://www.NameOfWebsite.gov

These letters represent the domain. A domain is the name of the company or organization represented by a particular website.

These letters stand for another domain. This domain is the Top Level Domain, or TLD. It describes the kind of site you are visiting. Here, *gov* stands for government. In other words, the site is sponsored by the government. There are other kinds of TLDs, too.

A website's address is called the Uniform or Universal Resource Locator, or URL. All URLs begin the same way—http://. This group of letters and symbols is followed by more letters and symbols. Look at the diagram. It shows the different parts of a website address.

No two websites have exactly the same URL. Each URL is registered, or recorded, by an organization called ICANN, or the Internet Corporation for Assigned Names and Numbers.

Thousands of URLs are registered every day. That's a lot of domain names. How can they all be different? Changing the TLD helps.

In the example URL http://www.NameOfWebsite.gov, the TLD .gov tells you that the website is a government site. The letters .com at the end of a URL tell you the website belongs to a business. If the address ends in .org, the website belongs to a research group or other organization. The letters .edu tell you the website is a school, college, or other educational website. A fun and informative government site is www.cia.gov/cia/publications/factbook/index.html. There, you can learn about and do research on different countries.

To meet the high demand for URLs, more domain names have been introduced. For example, you might see .info and .store at the end of a URL. Guess what these letters stand for. If you guessed information and store, you are right.

Domain names for websites outside the United States are different but simple to understand. Look at the last two letters in this URL: http://www.pm.gov.uk. The domain .uk stands for United Kingdom. Other country domains include .ca for Canada, .au for Australia, and .jp for Japan. You can travel around the world on the Web.

Doing research on the World Wide Web is a good way to supplement other kinds of research. There are many great informational websites about space and astronauts. Look at how the sample website is organized. (This is not a real website.)

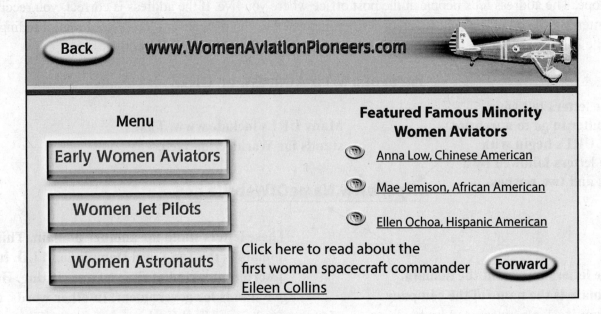

Hyperlinks are words or images that are underlined or highlighted. When you move your mouse over a hyperlink, the cursor will change form. When you click on the hyperlink, you will be taken to another web page with information on the same subject.

Answer the questions below about the information in the URL selection and information shown on the website example.

1. If a website is organized somewhat like an outline, what does the menu show?
   a. supporting details
   b. major topic headings
   c. title
   d. subheads

2. Who was the first woman spacecraft commander?
   a. Eileen Collins
   b. Ellen Ochoa
   c. Anna Low
   d. Mae Jemison

3. Who do you think was the first African American woman in space?
   a. Ellen Ochoa
   b. Anna Low
   c. Mae Jemison
   d. Eileen Collins

4. What is the website's address or URL?
   a. www.spacenews.edu
   b. www.featuredwomen.com
   c. www.Flygirls.org
   d. www.womenaviationpioneers.com

100

5. What are hyperlinks?

   a. websites that are run by NASA

   b. websites that are owned by the government

   c. words or images that can be clicked for more information

   d. words or images that are highlighted or underlined for artistic effect

6. What is a URL?

   a. a country abbreviation

   b. an abbreviation for the type of organization that sponsors the site

   c. a website address

   d. a domain name

7. What does *www* stand for in the URL?

   a. Who What Where   **c.** Web World Where

   b. Word Web World   **d.** World Wide Web

8. What does the TLD notation tell you at the end of a URL in the United States?

   a. the date the website was first posted   **c.** what kind of organization sponsors the site

   b. how many people created the site   **d.** what country the site originates from

9. What might the domain name represent on a commercial business site?

   a. the name of the sponsor   **c.** the name of the computer programmer

   b. the name of the business   **d.** the name of the owner of the business

10. What does *.gov* at the end of a URL show?

    a. that it is a nonprofit educational site   **c.** that it is a business-sponsored site

    b. that it is a government-sponsored site   **d.** that it is a foreign site

11. Who keeps track of all the domain names so that there are no duplicates?

    a. Universal Resource Locator

    b. Top Level Domain

    c. Internet Corporation for Assigned Names and Numbers, or ICANN

    d. World Wide Web

12. Where does the country abbreviation go on an international URL?

    a. at the end of the address

    b. in the middle of the address

    c. at the beginning of the address

    d. There is no country abbreviation.

101

Ⓒ **Read the biography of Ellen Ochoa.**

The First Hispanic American Woman in Space

Ellen Ochoa became an astronaut in 1991. She became the first Hispanic American woman in space in 1993. Since then, she has gone into space many times on the shuttle. In space, she has studied the effects of solar flare activity on Earth and Earth's atmosphere.

Ellen says life in space is very different from life on Earth. One huge difference is that there is no gravity in space. Gravity is the force that pulls things toward Earth. Gravity keeps us from flying off into space! In space, Ellen and the other astronauts have to learn how to float in zero gravity. In order to sleep, they tie their sleeping bags to a hook and float in their sleeping bags as they sleep.

Ellen Ochoa did not always want to be an astronaut. When she was a child, there were no women astronauts to follow. It did not seem like something girls did. Then, Ellen grew up and went to college and was exposed to women doing all kinds of interesting and valuable work. She did research in astrophysics and science at Stanford University.

Now, Ellen Ochoa has had an experience that not many people can claim. She has seen Earth from far away in space. She has trained hard with other astronauts to make sure that nothing goes wrong on their missions. In 2013, she became the director of NASA's Johnson Space Center in Houston, Texas.

Underline the correct answer to each question.

1. When did Ellen Ochoa first become an astronaut?

   a. 1981   **b.** 2001   **c.** 1991   **d.** 1999

2. What has she studied in space?

   a. the effects of gravity on astronauts   **c.** the effects of sleeping in space

   b. the effects of solar flares on Earth   **d.** the effects of going to college

3. How is life in space different from life on Earth?

   a. There is only liquid food in space.   **c.** There is zero gravity in space.

   b. There is no training in space.   **d.** There is no sleeping in space.

4. What is an example of gravity working?

   a. Astronauts tie their sleeping bags to a hook.

   b. A helium balloon is released.

   c. An apple falls from a tree.

   d. A puddle of water freezes.

5. Why is it important to have good role models?

   a. They show us we should not look too high.

   b. They can inspire us to do amazing things.

   c. They show us we can do things without working hard.

   d. They can help us set our sights low.

Selection 12

Solving the Garbage Problem

All across the United States, local governments are faced with the same growing problem—garbage. What is garbage? It's waste from our homes, businesses, schools, and hospitals. It's the stuff we don't need anymore. It's things we call useless. People in the United States produce nearly 250 million tons of solid waste each year! Then city governments must find places to store it.

Finding cheap landfills, or places to put our mounting trash, is only part of the problem. People who work in landfills want more money. Plus, some laws add to the cost of storing garbage. These laws are meant to keep groundwater safe and reduce methane, the dangerous gas that comes from landfills. But they also mean we pay more to have our trash picked up and hidden.

People argue about how to solve the garbage problem. Some think we should build more and bigger landfills. Others say we should build expensive power plants that burn trash for energy. However, many experts think that the best long-term answer is something called the triangle of the three *R*s. The three *R*s stand for *Reduce, Reuse, Recycle.* Together, the experts say, these three *R*s are a way to decrease our garbage problem.

Let's look at the first two *R*s in the triangle—*Reduce* and *Reuse*. We often overlook ways to reduce and reuse solid waste. But if we are going to manage our trash, reducing and reusing are more important than recycling. We reduce our trash when we buy and use fewer things. That's because in time, the things themselves become trash. So does the material that was used to wrap them.

Consider ways you can reduce your trash. One way is to buy concentrated items. For example, when you buy orange juice, buy the concentrated kind. Concentrated juice is usually packaged in a small, paper container. You add water at home. The people who sell unconcentrated juice add water before they package the juice. You pay extra for the water and the larger, plastic container used to hold it. Buying food or materials in bulk also cuts down on trash. When you buy one huge bag of rice, for example, you make less trash than when you buy more smaller bags.

Another way to reduce your trash is in your yard. There you can build a compost pile. Compost is a mix of food waste from your kitchen and cut grass and leaves from your yard. Stirring the compost helps it decay, or break down. Then you can add it to your yard or garden plants to help feed them and keep them moist. It also protects them from cold temperatures. Keeping a compost pile means usable plant waste stays at home instead of taking up space at a landfill.

Reusing is just as important as reducing the numbers of products we buy. Replace paper cups with china cups that can be used again and again. Carry cloth grocery bags to the grocery store. If you buy soda at the movies, pay attention to the specials. Some theaters sell plastic cups that you can use over and over again. And refills are cheaper.

Now let's look at the last *R* in the triangle—*Recycling*. Think for a moment about what you throw away in just one month. Chances are, if all of the trash you created were piled next to you, you would be standing next to a small mountain.

In 1988, the city of Phoenix paid for a garbage study. Leaders in the city wanted to know what people throw away. They hired Dr. Bill Rathje, of the University of Arizona Anthropology Department, to lead the study. Dr. Rathje and his team sorted and classified garbage from 500 homes. They learned that most of the garbage people threw away could be recycled. If we say that the trash in this study is like the trash we all throw away, almost 90 percent of the solid waste we create could be recycled. That means it never needs to reach the landfill!

We can throw out the garbage. We can carry it to the curb. We can even take it to the dump. But we can never really make our own mountains of garbage disappear. When we throw garbage away, it just goes somewhere else, and at a cost. Until we use the three *R*s, we are stuck with our trash.

Many cities are so short of landfill space that they give recycling bins to homes and businesses to shrink the amount of solid garbage waste they pick up. When you do something as simple as recycling a soda can, you help reduce the amount of aluminum that is taken from the ground. You also help reduce energy use and the water and air pollution that come from processing the aluminum.

In many older landfills, toxic, or poisonous, substances leak into the groundwater that we drink or use on our crops. Cleaning up these substances can be costly. Prevention makes more sense, and that's where recycling comes in. When you recycle motor oil, for example, you help keep toxic substances like lead out of your local landfill. That means you help keep them out of your air and water, too.

Of all the environmental problems we face, garbage is one problem you can really do something about. The choices you make every day affect the amount of garbage you throw away and the environmental problems you help create. When you follow the three *R*s—Reduce, Reuse, Recycle— you lessen waste and the problems that go with it. You save natural resources, decrease the need for energy, and reduce air, water, and land pollution. You also save money.

Garbage is everyone's problem, but you can be an important part of the solution. Following the three *R*s saves money, benefits the environment, and protects your health. So start using the three *R*s to manage your own mountain of garbage. Conquer your mountain with a cry of "Reduce, Reuse, Recycle" that can be heard around the world.

Any ideas?

Describe on another sheet of paper what you and your family can do to keep the planet clean. What ideas from the selection could you put in place? What other ideas do you have for reducing garbage and the problem of landfills?

Name _____ Date _____

A Underline the correct answer to each question.

1. How many tons of solid waste do people in the United States produce each year?

   a. 201 million tons   **c.** 250 million tons

   b. 300 million tons   **d.** 500 million tons

2. What adds to the cost of landfills?

   a. new trucks for recycling

   b. higher pay for landfill workers and new environmental laws

   c. special exhaust systems for the garbage trucks used

   d. the kind of dirt that is taken out of the landfill

3. What kind of dangerous gas can come out of landfills?

   a. helium   **c.** gasoline

   b. oxygen   **d.** methane

4. According to this selection, what are some other ways people want to get rid of trash?

   a. burn it in power plants

   b. bury it in their back yards

   c. send it on a ship to poorer countries

   d. put it inside of an extinct volcano

5. What is the triangle of the three *R*s?

   a. Refuse, Renew, Redo   **c.** Reduce, Reuse, Recycle

   b. Resell, Repel, Remake   **d.** Resist, Reject, React

6. How can we reduce our trash?

   a. buy and use fewer things

   b. put our trash in our neighbor's bin

   c. eat less and make our parents eat more

   d. put the trash out less often

7. What is mixed with food waste to create compost?

   a. plastic wrappers   **c.** wooden posts

   b. cut grass and leaves   **d.** glass bottles and caps

8. How much solid waste did the trash study report that people in the United States could recycle?

   a. 50 percent of solid waste

   b. 90 percent of solid waste

   c. 60 percent of solid waste

   d. 100 percent of solid waste

B Refer to the bar graph to answer the questions below.

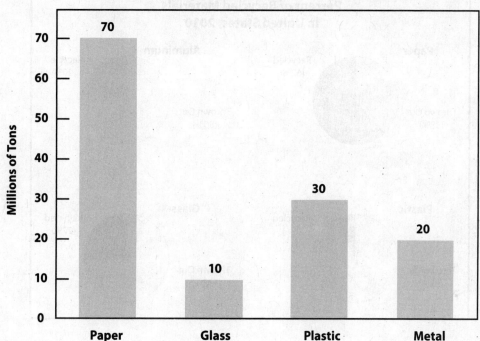

Materials Disposed of in the United States, 2010

1. In 2010, people in the United States threw out how many tons of paper?

   a. 7 million

   b. 0.7 million

   c. 30 million

   d. 70 million

2. According to the graph, how many tons of glass and metal were thrown out?

   a. 10 million

   b. 20 million

   c. 30 million

   d. 50 million

3. Which of the following would be another good title for the graph?

   a. How to Recycle Materials

   b. Types of Trash

   c. Too Much Plastic

   d. Metals and Other Materials

4. What can you conclude from the information in the graph?

   a. People use more paper than glass.

   b. It costs more to throw away metal than glass.

   c. People should write more letters.

   d. People should buy more paper.

C **Refer to the circle graphs to answer the questions below.**

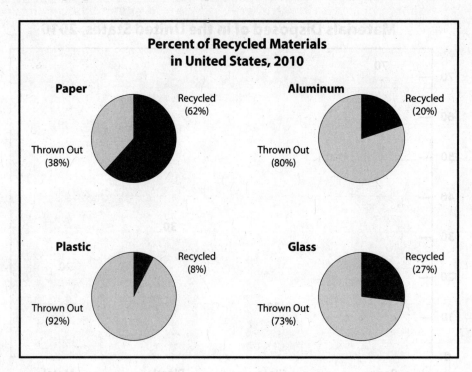

**Percent of Recycled Materials
in United States, 2010**

Paper
Recycled (62%)
Thrown Out (38%)

Aluminum
Recycled (20%)
Thrown Out (80%)

Plastic
Recycled (8%)
Thrown Out (92%)

Glass
Recycled (27%)
Thrown Out (73%)

1. Which of the following materials has been most successfully recycled?

   a. paper

   b. aluminum

   c. plastic

   d. glass

2. From the information in the circle graphs, what can you conclude?

   a. Most glass is recycled.

   b. Paper is easier to recycle than plastic.

   c. People use more plastic than glass.

   d. Most communities recycle.

3. What percentage of glass is thrown out?

   a. 27%   **c.** 73%

   b. 38%   **d.** 80%

4. What percentage of aluminum is recycled?

   a. 20%   **c.** 73%

   b. 27%   **d.** 80%

Name _____ Date _____

D Write an outline on the lines below of the selection "Solving the Garbage Problem." Write the main ideas and important details. Remember to use Roman numerals in your outline.

_____

_____

_____

_____

_____

_____

_____

_____

_____

_____

_____

_____

_____

_____

_____

_____

_____

_____

_____

_____

_____

_____

109

Selection 12

Core Skills Reading Comprehension, Grade 8

E Use your outline from page 109 to write a summary of the selection. Remember that a summary should include the most important main ideas and details. Do not include your opinions about the selection.

_____

_____

_____

_____

_____

_____

_____

_____

_____

_____

_____

_____

_____

_____

_____

_____

_____

_____

_____

_____

_____

_____

Skills Review: Selections 7–12

A **Read the selection below. The author is trying to convince you to see a movie. Underline each persuasive argument you find.**

A Story for the Ages

Most of the time, I'm disappointed when I see a movie based on one of my favorite books. But *To Kill a Mockingbird* didn't disappoint me at all. In fact, I think everyone should see it. After they read the book, that is.

Made in 1962, the movie is in black and white, but don't let that stop you from seeing it. In some ways, the black and white colors help tell the story in a very artistic way. For example, the colors create the movie's setting. The story happens in the early 1930s during the Great Depression. Times were hard for many people. There weren't enough jobs and many people were poor. You could say that the movie's plain colors help tell the story of *To Kill a Mockingbird* in a beautiful and visual way.

The black and white colors also stand for the struggle between people. For example, the story shows how different life was for black and white people living in the South in the 1930s. The struggle between prejudice and tolerance is highlighted in a fascinating way that will keep you watching.

The Finch family lives in a small town in Alabama. Atticus Finch is a lawyer. A black man is accused of a crime he didn't commit. He's too poor to hire a lawyer, so the judge in the case assigns one. Ordinarily, that might not be difficult, but because the accused man is black as well as poor, the judge must choose carefully. He asks Atticus. Atticus believes in justice and takes the case because it's the right thing to do. However, some people who live in his town don't agree. They threaten him and his children, Jem and Scout.

Scout is six years old and she is a wonderful, spunky character. She is the movie's narrator, that is, she tells the story. Jem is her older brother. When the story begins, school is out. Scout and Jem meet Dill, a boy Scout's age who's visiting his aunt for part of the summer. Together, the children look for interesting ways to fill hot and lazy summer days.

The children spend time in their treehouse telling stories. One of those stories is about a run-down house nearby and the people who live there. Here is an example of another struggle. This time it's a struggle between truth and lies. The children learn that what they believe about Mr. Radley, the man who owns the house, and his son, Boo, isn't true. At first, Boo is a frightening mystery. This mystery heightens the power of the movie. Then something awful happens and the children learn that Boo is their friend.

The children believe that Boo is crazy and that his father keeps him locked away. Consequently, the children are afraid to go near the house. One day, Scout, who is rolling inside a rubber tire, accidentally goes into the Radleys' yard. The tire hits the front steps and Scout is too dizzy and too frightened to move. Jem rushes in to save her. Later, when Scout really does need help, it won't be Jem who protects her. It will be Boo.

It is Atticus's work that brings Boo outside to help Scout. While the children are solving the mystery of who is hiding small gifts in a tree, their father is defending his client, Tom Robinson. Feelings in the town are strong and set against Atticus and Tom. But Atticus doesn't back down, and matters get worse. Someone attacks Scout, and Boo must kill someone to save her.

This movie is one of the best movies ever made. First, it was based on an award-winning book by Harper Lee. She won the Pulitzer Prize for her book in 1961. Then, the movie was nominated for several Academy Awards in 1963, including Best Picture. But it's not the awards alone that make this movie worth seeing. Watch this movie because it tells a timeless story. It's a story that shows the opposites that exist in the world. It shows love and hate and truth and lies. It shows fear and bravery and right from wrong. Finally, it helps us see ourselves as the people we are and the people we can be. See *To Kill a Mockingbird* and I think you'll agree.

B **Summarize the movie's plot. Include only facts about the movie. Do not include the writer's opinions.**

_____

_____

_____

_____

_____

_____

_____

_____

_____

_____

C Underline the correct answer to each question.

1. When and where do the story and movie take place?

    a. the 1960s during a peace demonstration

    b. the 1940s during World War II

    c. the 1930s during the Great Depression

    d. the 1980s in a corporate office

2. How do the black and white colors of the film help tell the story?

    a. They highlight the lighthearted story.

    b. They reflect the harsh, bleak times.

    c. They contrast with the musical theme of the movie.

    d. They emphasize the costumes of the dancers.

3. Who is the narrator of the movie's story?

    a. the older brother, Jem   **c.** a crazy man named Boo

    b. the lawyer, Atticus   **d.** a six-year-old named Scout

4. Who wrote the book that the movie is based on?

    a. Atticus Finch   **c.** Tom Robinson

    b. Harper Lee   **d.** Boo Radley

5. Who is on trial?

    a. Tom Robinson   **c.** Atticus Finch

    b. Boo Radley   **d.** Jem Finch

6. What prize did the author of the book win?

    a. Pulitzer Prize   **c.** Nobel Prize

    b. Newbery Award   **d.** Caldecott Award

7. Why does the reviewer urge the reader to see the movie?

    a. because it is a popular, upbeat story

    b. because it is an action-packed thriller

    c. because it is a timeless story

    d. because it is a wonderful romance

8. Why does the reviewer relate so much of the story?

    a. to impress the reader

    b. to interest the reader

    c. to help the reader with a book report

    d. to confuse the reader

Name _____ Date _____

D Look at the circle graph and answer the questions.

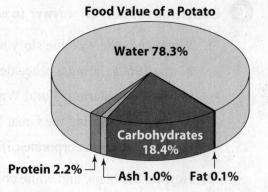

Food Value of a Potato

Water 78.3%

Carbohydrates 18.4%

Protein 2.2% Ash 1.0% Fat 0.1%

1. How much of a potato is water?
   a. 10%
   b. 70.4%
   c. 78.3%
   d. 18.4%

2. How much of a potato is protein?
   a. 78.3%
   b. 2.2%
   c. 0.1%
   d. 1.0%

3. After water, what makes up the next highest percentage of a potato?
   a. ash
   b. fat
   c. protein
   d. carbohydrates

4. What makes up the smallest percentage of a potato?
   a. ash
   b. protein
   c. fat
   d. water

E Choose a word to complete each sentence.

apparel	unvarying	mummified
resin	accomplishments	mounted
landfill	drought	prosperous
agricultural	candidate	bandwagon

1. A person running for political office is called a _____.

2. Ancient Egyptian priests _____ bodies.

3. Another word for a trash dump is a _____.

4. Clothes are also called _____.

5. A long period without rain is a _____.

6. Products related to farming are _____.

7. Something that does not change is _____.

8. A wealthy successful person is _____.

F Circle the correct analogy.

1. *Parents* are to *chores* as *teachers* are to _____.

   homework   baby-sitting   parents

2. *President* is to *vice-president* as *superintendent* is to _____.

   janitor   teacher   principal

3. *Teachers* are to *students* as *parents* are to _____.

   pets   children   grandparents

4. *Musicians* are to *music* as *athletes* are to _____.

   baseball   sports   soccer

5. *Creative* is to *dull* as *positive* is to _____.

   negative   joyful   deep

G Read this poem and answer the questions about poetic comparisons.

Homework

I plow in as soon as I hit the door
of home. Well, first I have to fuel up
with snacks and drink.
Then, I sink into a mountain of papers.
Sometimes I wonder, are we all invisible vapors—
ghosts, the teachers do not see?
Perhaps they do not know how much they each
have assigned us to complete?
This feat, this mountain of papers,
Will I reach the top?

---

1. Why does the poet use the word *plow*?

   _____

2. What is the poet comparing the load of homework to?

   _____

3. What is the poet comparing to "invisible vapors" or "ghosts"?

   _____

4. What is the "feat" the poet is probably talking about?

   _____

H Use the bar graph and the paragraph to answer the questions.

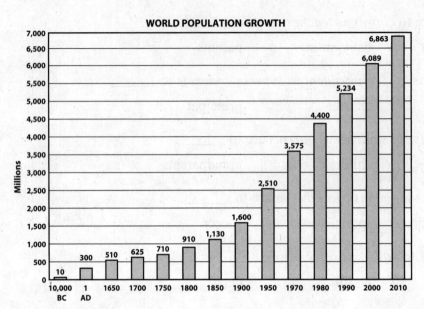

WORLD POPULATION GROWTH

In 1994, the world's population growth reached 5.6 billion people. By the year 2020, the population is expected to rise to 7.6 billion. Most of the population increase will take place in developing countries. In fact, of the 2.3 billion people added to the population, 9 out of 10 will be from developing nations.

1. By the year 2020, what is the world's population expected to increase to?

   a. 2.3 billion

   b. 5.6 billion

   c. 7.6 billion

   d. 13.5 billion

2. Which of the following is the main idea of the paragraph?

   a. Developing nations are growing rapidly.

   b. The world's population is increasing.

   c. World population growth is a problem.

   d. In 1994, the world's population was 5.6 billion people.

3. According to the bar graph, which statement below is true?

   a. World population was 300 million in the year AD 1.

   b. Population doubled between 1800 and 1900.

   c. In 1900, there were under one million people in the world.

   d. In 10,000 BC, there were about 10,000 people in the world.

4. In 1700, how many million people were there in the world?

   a. 510   **b.** 710   **c.** 625   **d.** 300

5. What do you think is meant by the phrase *developing nations*?

   a. established countries like the U.S.

   b. South American countries

   c. members of the United Nations

   d. poor countries wanting to become more advanced

116

Answer Key

Selection 1
pages 1–7

A
1. c   5. d
2. a   6. b
3. c   7. a
4. b   8. c

B Check that the summary includes the significant events of the selection in sequence, with the important lesson clearly represented.

C
1. glossy   7. observation
2. boredom   8. confer
3. nearsighted   9. reflex
4. pathetic   10. obvious
5. prejudice   11. snickered
6. snob   12. deflated

D
1. M
2. S
3. M
4. S
5. S
6. M

Selection 2
pages 8–18

A
1. c   5. a
2. b   6. b
3. c   7. a
4. d   8. d

B
1. orchid   7. frolicking
2. atlas   8. poisonous
3. rehearsed   9. fantasy
4. bamboo   10. noticeable
5. flexible   11. tomb
6. typhoon   12. eventually

C
1. Northern Hemisphere
2. Japan
3. Pacific
4. Asia
5. Tropical; hilly with bamboo forests; exotic tombs
6. The Far East; Asia

D
1. a, c, d, f, g
2. Answers will vary.
3. a, d, e, f
4. b, c, e

E Paragraph 1: D, M, D. Paragraph 2: M, D, D. Paragraph 3: D, M, D, D. Paragraph 4: D, M, D. Paragraph 5: M, D, D.

F Another Kind of Language (Outline)
I.
  A.
    2. By 1990, the number was almost 800,000.
    3. After 2010, the Korean American population was over 1.7 million.
  B.
    2. Korean American families must deal with different ideas about what is good behavior.
    3. Because they want freedom and stability, they try to bridge the gap between the two cultures.
II.
  A.
    2. Misunderstandings have sometimes happened because of differences in customs and beliefs.
    3. Community leaders have brought the two sides together.
  B.
    1. Korean Americans are not comfortable smiling unless something is funny.
    2. Looking someone directly in the eyes is bad manners.
    3. Physical contact in public is bad manners.

G
1. It is better to blend into society than stand out.
2. He received the news and ran off impulsively without thinking.
3. She felt she had been sent on a fruitless search.
4. Sarah's mom was watching us very closely.
5. Be honest and truthful and don't swerve into doing wrong.
6. The cowboy was feeling very down and depressed.

Selection 3
pages 19–27

A
1. d   5. c
2. c   6. d
3. b   7. a
4. a   8. c

B
1. a, e, f, g
2. a, d, g
3. b, c, d

C
1. united—dissolved
2. flexible—unchangeable
3. exhibit—hide
4. inhale—exhale
5. translucent—darkened
6. prejudiced—fair
7. inflate—deflate

8. frolicked—sat still
9. fantasy—reality
10. aloof—friendly
11. depressed—cheerful

D 1. parlor   6. skyscrapers
     2. comedian   7. exhibit
     3. chronicles   8. neon
     4. depressed   9. dissolve
     5. translucent   10. arcade

E 1. b
     2. a
     3. b
     4. c
     5. d

F 1. F   5. O
     2. O   6. F
     3. F   7. F
     4. F   8. O

Selection 4
pages 28–34

A 1. b   5. c
     2. c   6. a
     3. b   7. c
     4. d

B 1. M   7. M
     2. S   8. S
     3. S   9. S
     4. M   10. M
     5. S   11. S
     6. S

C Answers will vary. Possible answers are given.
     1. argued   5. curled up
     2. expectant   6. scratched
     3. cut off   7. mean
     4. wrestled   8. jumped

D 1. rest—pine tree
     2. trail—deer trail
     3. thirst—half-full
     4. leader—Ms. Reeves
     5. best friend—Jada
     6. Once Yuki found her "bald tree" in the distance, she would take sightings on landmarks between where she was standing and the tree. Once she would arrive at the middle landmark, she would take another sighting and find another landmark in line with her tree, until she was able to make her way to the pine.

Selection 5
pages 35–43

A 1. d   5. d
     2. a   6. d
     3. c   7. b
     4. b

B 1. permanent—lasting
     2. resume—start again
     3. intended—meant
     4. vicious—mean
     5. fought—quarreled
     6. fumbled—acted clumsy
     7. abandoned—left behind
     8. happy—lighthearted
     9. affirming—positive
     10. pretend—imaginary
     11. align—line up

C 1. reassemble   6. reactor
     2. outcropping   7. retrace
     3. deliberately   8. digital
     4. weatherproof   9. parched
     5. canopy   10. desperately

D 1. b   5. d
     2. a   6. d
     3. c   7. d
     4. d   8. b

E 3, 5, 8, 1, 4, 6, 2, 7, 9, The dog took it and buried it in the yard.

Selection 6
pages 44–51

A 1. a
     2. a
     3. d
     4. b
     5. b
     6. a
     7. c

B 1. a
     2. b
     3. b

C Answers will vary. Possible answers follow:
first statement: "Please, God, make him think I'm still pretty," "I had my hair cut off and sold it because I couldn't have lived through Christmas without giving you a present."
second statement: "Poor fellow, he was only twenty-two . . . " "And here I have lamely related to you the uneventful chronicle of two foolish children . . ."

118

third statement: "Of all who give and receive gifts, such as they are the wisest." "They are the magi."

fourth statement: "shabby little couch," "the income was shrunk," "He needed a new overcoat, and he was without gloves."

D 1. Answers will vary. Sample answer: "The Gift of the Magi" has a narrator and a plot. "To My Dear and Loving Husband" rhymes and has short lines.

2. Answers will vary. Sample answer: "I prize thy love more than whole Mines of gold," "Or all the riches that the East doth hold." "Nor ought but love from thee give recompense." "Thy love is such I can no way repay."

3. Della and Jim try to buy gifts that show how much they love each other, but the gifts are of no use to them. They end up without their treasures, but their love remains strong.

4. thoughtful, formal, hopeful

Skills Review: Selections 1–6
pages 52–58

A Underline:

Paragraph 1: A unique way to capture your memories is with a time capsule.

Paragraph 2: Select a box or container to hold the things that you will place in your time capsule.

Paragraph 3: Find things to put in your time capsule that you think represent your life now.

Paragraph 4: After that, make a final decision about where you want to place your time capsule.

Paragraph 5: You must decide on a date when you want the time capsule to be opened.

Paragraph 6: You might want to create your time capsule with a friend or a group of friends.

1. You must decide on a date when you want the time capsule to be opened.
2. c
3. c
4. d
5. a
6. a
7. Answers will vary

B Paragraph 1—g   Paragraph 5—d
   Paragraph 2—c   Paragraph 6—e
   Paragraph 3—b   Paragraph 7—f
   Paragraph 4—a

C Answers will vary. Some example answers are:
   Cause: park unsafe; Effect: Julie fell.
   Cause: letter to the mayor; Effect: park repaired
   Cause: park repaired; Effect: friends go for a run

D Check that the summary includes the significant events in the biography and is organized in a thoughtful way, with the main ideas and important details clearly presented.

E 1. dull—glossy
   2. obvious—hidden
   3. friendly—snobbish
   4. bored—eager
   5. wise—foolish
   6. common—unique
   7. restrict—free
   8. pored over—scanned
   9. canopy—roots
   10. provoke—soothe
   11. sit up—recline

F 1. glumly—sadly
   2. chattered—talked
   3. reassemble—rebuild
   4. chronicled—reported
   5. litter—trash
   6. aching—hurting
   7. pick up—gather
   8. avoid—go around
   9. weatherproof—protect
   10. incredible—fantastic
   11. scrunched—crumpled

G 1. b
   2. a
   3. c
   4. c
   5. d

Selection 7
pages 59–70

A 1. a   5. b
   2. d   6. b
   3. d   7. d
   4. a   8. c

B How English and Western Styles of Riding Are Alike:
   Both have a long, interesting history.
   Both have benefited from inventions.
   Both have their own special tack and clothing.

How English and Western Styles of Riding Are Different:
   English riding came to America from England, while Western riding originated in northern Mexico and in the southwestern United States.
   English riding has a traditional, social purpose, while Western riding began for working purposes.

119

In English riding, the rider sits up straight and
tall; in Western riding, the rider may slouch
down for comfort during work.

English riders wear traditional clothes, while
Western riders wear casual work clothes.

The English saddle has no horn, is simple and
light, and is designed for easy jumping. The
Western saddle is strong and has a saddle horn,
which is used to rope and pull.

In English riding, both hands hold the reins. In
Western riding, the rider holds the reins in
one hand.

C 1. c
2. b
3. c
4. d
5. Both bars would be shorter than the bar for
"Recreation."

D 1. her saddle
2. English-style dressage riding
3. The poet is on a cattle drive.
4. herd/heard
5. to communicate the formal posture and air that is
a part of English-style riding

E 1. sheep   6. climbing
2. tree   7. technology
3. sloppy   8. eating
4. horse   9. stable
5. people

F 1. The measurement was <u>precise</u> because all the
numbers were carefully defined.
2. The fashion model wore the latest <u>apparel</u>.
3. After riding, she carefully put away all the
riding <u>tack</u>.
4. He had jumped his horse over the trimmed
<u>hedges</u>.
5. Ancient <u>nomads</u> found ways to improve
horseback riding.
6. The well-trained horse made the <u>intricate</u>
movements look easy.

G 1. exact   5. unvarying
2. defined   6. distinct
3. neat   7. measured
4. accurate   8. strict

H 1. c   5. b
2. b   6. d
3. c   7. b
4. c

Selection 8
pages 71–78

A 1. c   5. d
2. b   6. a
3. d   7. c
4. b   8. a

B Underline:
Paragraph 1—This shows the importance of
religion in Egyptian culture.
Paragraph 2—Pyramids were huge tombs built
for kings.
Paragraph 3—Egyptians believed that they needed
to be buried with things they could use in the
afterlife.
Paragraph 4—Some of the most exciting
archaeological finds are tombs.
Paragraph 5—Scientists study the paintings to
learn about Egyptian beliefs.
Paragraph 6—The unopened tomb helped
archaeologists learn how Egyptian kings
were buried.
Egyptian Mummies and Culture (Outline)
Check to see that the outline is organized in
a thoughtful way, with the main ideas and
important details clearly presented.

C   **Across**   **Down**
1. pyramid   2. adults
3. embalm   5. mummified
4. steam   7. panels
6. mummy   9. enter
8. linen
10. natron
11. sick

D 1. mummies   5. process
2. embalm   6. interfere
3. glaciers   7. intestines
4. bacteria   8. preserved

Selection 9
pages 79–84

A 1. a
2. c
3. a
4. c
5. b
6. c
7. b

B 1. without reason
2. world-wide problems
3. inform and persuade

120

C 1. commodities
2. agricultural
3. drought
4. prosperous
5. consumption
6. imported

D 1. fiction; green Oltrons from outer space
2. fact
3. fiction; UFO sighting
4. fiction; President Barack Obama
5. fact
6. fact
7. fiction; acre cost one million dollars; West was never settled

Selection 10
pages 85–94

A 1. c
2. a
3. c
4. d
5. b
6. d
7. d

B 1. mounted
2. dividends
3. delirious
4. adequate
5. surplus

C 1. Corporations made huge profits.
2. People didn't have money to spend on goods.
3. Bankers called in loans.

D 1. 2
2. 3
3. 1
4. 1
5. 2
6. 3
7. 2
8. 1
9. insist on
10. actor Brad Jones
11. fun-filled
12. is lightning fast

E 1. d
2. a
3. d
4. d
5. b
6. a
7. b
8. a
9. c
10. b

F Check ads 4, 6, 8, 9, and 11.

G 1. Hoover
2. Roosevelt
3. Hoover
4. Roosevelt
5. Hoover
6. Roosevelt
7. Hoover
8. Hoover
9. Roosevelt
10. Roosevelt

H Hoover uses complicated language (such as "The cumulative effects of demoralizing price falls . . .") and long sentences. Roosevelt uses simpler, shorter sentences such as "You know the story" and "And there we are today." Answers will vary about which style is more effective. Students may think Hoover sounds more confident or Roosevelt is clearer.

I 1. worldwide
2. prosperity
3. broken
4. responsibility
5. recovered
6. imported
7. fear
8. outside
9. speculation
10. suffered

Selection 11
pages 95–102

A 1. b
2. c
3. d
4. b
5. c
6. a
7. c
8. a

B 1. b
2. a
3. c
4. d
5. c
6. c
7. d
8. c
9. b
10. b
11. c
12. a

C 1. c
2. b
3. c
4. c
5. b

Selection 12
pages 103–110

A
1. c
2. b
3. d
4. a
5. c
6. a
7. b
8. b

B
1. d
2. c
3. b
4. a

C
1. a
2. b
3. c
4. a

D Make sure students have included all the main ideas and details. Students do not need to include every paragraph in their outline, just the ones with the most important details.

E Check that the summary includes the significant facts presented in the report and is organized in a thoughtful way, with the main ideas and important details clearly expressed. The summary should not include the student's opinions.

Skills Review: Selections 7–12
pages 111–116

A Underline:
1. In some ways, the black and white colors help tell the story in a very artistic way.
2. You could say that the movie's plain colors help tell the story of *To Kill a Mockingbird* in a beautiful and visual way.
3. The struggle between prejudice and tolerance is highlighted in a fascinating way that will keep you watching.
4. Scout is six years old and she is a wonderful, spunky character.
5. This mystery heightens the power of the movie.
6. This movie is one of the best movies ever made.
7. First, it was based on an award-winning book by Harper Lee.
8. Then, the movie was nominated for several Academy Awards in 1963, including Best Picture.
9. Watch this movie because it tells a timeless story.

B Check that the summary includes the important elements of the plot.

C
1. c
2. b
3. d
4. b
5. a
6. a
7. c
8. b

D
1. c
2. b
3. d
4. c

E
1. candidate
2. mummified
3. landfill
4. apparel
5. drought
6. agricultural
7. unvarying
8. prosperous

F
1. homework
2. principal
3. children
4. sports
5. negative

G
1. The word *plow* brings to mind the idea of hard work.
2. a mountain
3. the students
4. homework

H
1. c
2. a
3. a
4. c
5. d